VOICES FROM
THE
HOLOCAUST

VOICES FROM
THE
HOLOCAUST

Harry James Cargas

THE UNIVERSITY PRESS OF KENTUCKY

Copyright © 1993 by The University Press of Kentucky

Scholarly publisher for the Commonwealth,
serving Bellarmine College, Berea College, Centre
College of Kentucky, Eastern Kentucky University,
The Filson Club, Georgetown College, Kentucky
Historical Society, Kentucky State University,
Morehead State University, Murray State University,
Northern Kentucky University, Transylvania University,
University of Kentucky, University of Louisville,
and Western Kentucky University.

Editorial and Sales Offices: Lexington, Kentucky 40508-4008

Library of Congress Cataloging-in-Publication Data

Cargas, Harry J.
    Voices from the Holocaust / Harry James Cargas.
        p.   cm.
    ISBN 0-8131-1802-6; 0-8131-0825-X (acid-free paper)
    1. Holocaust survivors—Interviews.   2. Holocaust, Jewish
(1939-1945)—Influence.   I. Title.
D804.3.C35   1993
940.53'18—dc20   92-20178

CONTENTS

PREFACE

To the extent that the interviews appearing in this book are successful, a measure of trust between the conversants may be presumed by the reader. That each of the participants accorded me his or her trust is in every case a gift I treasure. To reflect on the thought that each of these people with whom I talked is a friend is a satisfaction undeserved but deeply appreciated.

Many volumes of interviews on the Shoah have been published—compilations centering on a single theme: survivors, their children, even children of Nazis. This work has a wider scope. Here, major figures of the Holocaust, some more directly involved in the actual Event than others, all of whom have reflected on its significance from a variety of valuable perspectives (law, theology, philosophy, literature, memorialization), speak their minds, their hearts. I gratefully express my appreciation for their willingness to share and my appreciation for who they are.

Sharon Hessler's contribution to the completion of this book goes far beyond typing. Her smile and her friendship have been a great asset to me, and to Sharon I want to acknowledge a sincere "Thank you."

The interview with Dorothee Soelle was published in *Encounter*, volume 49, Spring 1988. The interview with Leon Wells was published in *Bridges*, volume 1, Fall/Winter 1989. The Leo Eitinger interview was published in *Martyrdom and Resistance*, November to December 1983.

For EDDY L. HARRIS

"One friend in a lifetime is much."
—*Henry Brooks Adams*

INTRODUCTION

For many years I have been studying the Holocaust from various perspectives. I did so first as a father, next as a Christian, third as a student, now as a writer and teacher. The event has overwhelmed my thinking in all of these areas. I would not have it any other way. Although I did not realize that a pattern to my thinking was evolving, it seems that one of the constants in my approaching history has been this: What has it meant for me? Whether I read a play by Sophocles, learn that Giordano Bruno was burned at the stake, imagine the terrors of Genghis Kahn, study the life of Lucretia Borgia, try to understand Martin Luther's frustrations, look at the collaboration of certain African leaders in the slave trade, try to cope with the conquistadors, become more aware of the Innuits in northern Canada, I ask myself how I am affected— and if there is some way I ought to be responding. This book is one response I make to the Holocaust and the evils that it implies.

I was twenty-eight when I first became aware of the Holocaust, and it hit me in both a devastating and a liberating way. I had become a father a second time. We had moved to New York City (I'm originally from Hamtramck, Michigan, then a rugged section of Detroit), and my idea of being a husband and father was corrupted by what I now call the John Wayne

School of Charm: the macho figure of the family had to be tough, show no emotion, never admit to being wrong, show confidence in everything he did. I was teaching and the athletic director at St. David's School (a school for boys) in Manhattan. The father of one of the children edited *Jubilee*, a Catholic magazine of some excellence. The editor, Ed Rice, had been a college roommate of Thomas Merton, the monk and best-selling author. One Saturday I picked up a copy of the periodical, and that issue contained an excerpt from Elie Wiesel's memoir *Night*. It was the section in which the young boy, Elie, saw his father beaten to death in Auschwitz. It changed my life.

I was staggered to read of a boy still loving his father even though the father was helpless to protect his child. I must have been thinking that John Wayne would never have let this happen, while Shlomo Wiesel did. And still Elie loved the man. Was there a possibility that my children could continue to love me if I showed weakness, if I failed at something, if I were humiliated in public?

So I began to devour as many nonfiction books as I could on the Holocaust to see if family relationships among Jews were somehow different from what I thought that they "ought" to be. The tragedy of the Shoah began to be imprinted on my soul, slowly, but I was also being liberated from my own concept of fatherhood, which was so monumentally deficient.

And as I read, I became more aware of the Holocaust as a Christian, particularly as a Catholic. One day it became apparent to me, in a way it had not earlier, that every killer of Jews, of Gypsies, of Jehovah's Witnesses, of homosexuals was a baptized Christian. It takes a lot of people to kill a lot of people—and the murderers, the traitors, the profiteers, the onlookers all had Christian backgrounds. What did that mean for me, for someone who presumed to take his religious commitment seriously?

Next, I studied the Holocaust and World War II in order to know the circumstances better, circumstances that took place during my lifetime but of which I was totally unaware.

I remember interviewing a dying Holocaust survivor in the 1970s—he had asked me to write his autobiography for him—and he told me that he read as much as he could about the Holocaust because he wanted to try to learn what was happening while he was in a death camp, ignorant of anything beyond what he could actually see for himself. I felt at one time that I, too, was imprisoned in ignorance about the tragedy and tried to make up for it in an almost obsessive way.

Finally, I came to teach and write about the Holocaust. The impetus stemmed from an interview I did with Elie Wiesel for my television program *Continuum* on the Central Education Network. When he arrived for the taping (some twenty years ago, now) the cameras were not ready and he had to talk with me for forty-five minutes. For me it was a mystical moment. A week later I wrote to him asking if he would be interested in collaborating on a dialogue book. He agreed. (The result, *Conversations with Elie Wiesel*, greatly updated and rereleased in 1992 by Justice Books, is hardly a dialogue work but more a question/answer volume.)

Since then I have published many articles and seven more volumes on the Holocaust, particularly on Christian responsibility regarding the topic, given many lectures, conducted many courses, and attended and organized many conferences dealing with the event. In doing so, I came to meet many of the important figures who have themselves written and spoken from their experiences so eloquently. Some are represented in this book.

What I have tried to do here is cover as much of the diversity of the Shoah as I could. This is an attempt to present as full a picture as possible of what happened and how it is thought about from the perspective of the survivor, the underground fighter, the rescuer, the prosecutor, the writer, the Christian theologian, the philosopher, and the psychologist. While this is a widely cast net, I was, understandably, unable to include any perpetrators or onlookers in this "catch."

All of the people included can be described as participants in the events here discussed. From that perspective, they have unique points of view to share with us. As we get further from the Second World War, fewer "participants" will be available to tell their stories. Certain historians strongly oppose eye-witness accounts, claiming that memory lapses, time, and egos weaken the reliability of such testimonies. Only documents, they insist, are reliable.

As may be obvious, this is a very personal book, which initially may be a surprising comment. In one way, interviews, like photographs, are often used to distance oneself from the subject at hand. They can be a method of not getting involved. Susan Sontag has written incisively on the use of the camera for such purpose in *On Photography*. For me, however, interviewing is a way of becoming *more* involved with the subject and with the person interviewed.

In a cab ride some years ago from Vienna to Prague with the late novelist Borden Deal, Kurt Vonnegut and I got into a discussion of his idea of what an extended family might be. He was using it in the work of fiction he was then writing, *Slapstick*. Vonnegut said that everybody should be randomly given new middle names, such as "daffodil" or "buttercup"—50,000 people with the same new name throughout the United States. When you traveled, in whatever city you found yourself, you would find, in a special section of the phone book, someone (or several persons) with your assigned moniker. You'd have instant family, people you could call on wherever you were.

My response was to say that my extended family all live on the shelves in my den and most are deceased. I think of Plato and Dante and Catherine of Siena and Leonardo and Teilhard de Chardin and James Baldwin and Yasunari Kawabata and Eleanor Roosevelt and Aleksandr Solzhenitsyn as not only family members but very reliable ones. They are always found where I last left them, they say wonderful and important things to me, they instruct me without ever speaking harsh words directly to me, are never impatient with my shortcomings. They are my way of becoming involved with the history and the culture of our planet. But of course they can respond to me only in limited ways—as when they give me new insights because current thinking and events add to the meanings of their works and lives or because I have grown in some manner and understand better what they were about.

With the Holocaust survivors and others less directly involved in the Shoah my relationship can be much more intimate. We are contemporaries. I have studied the subject in greater depth than I have most other topics. It has an enormously powerful grip on me. I can encounter these figures face to face, see them smile, fidget, become absorbed in memories, discover new meanings for their experiences even as we are together. I become immersed in one of history's most awesome events—and one so profoundly important to me personally—in a measure of totality. It is one thing to read a survivor's revelation that she lost eighty-five of her family to the Nazis. It is another thing to see and hear her tell you personally of that pain. It is one thing to read a writer's novel or document, quite another to have him tell you the circumstances surrounding what and why he wrote.

Perhaps several themes may be seen running through these pages. Death and rebirth might be one. Another could have something to do with the humility of each of the interviewees, every one of whom is in a certain way to be perceived as heroic. What I would like to focus on briefly, for the reader to watch for in this volume, is what can be called the implicit theodicy of each of those represented here. A rather technical term, theodicy has to do with the theology of evil which is implied by each of my respondents, whether each is a believer, an agnostic, or an atheist.

Throughout history people have regarded evil in various ways. It has been seen as real or illusory; as punishment, purifying, random, deserved (or not), a sign of indifference or incompetence on the part of God or Nature. But a whole new dimension, or at least emphasis, on the problem of evil has resulted from the Holocaust experience.

Arnost Lustig, through his writings and in his interview here, rebels against an evil he knows is there. Most (though not all) survivors do not question the reality of evil, but many disagree as to its nature. Simon Wiesenthal tries to balance the evil he saw with justice and attempts to do so without a trace of hatred. For Leon Wells, the evil of World War II has led him to the conclusion that no God he knows of can have allowed the Holocaust, so his unbelief follows from that.

Resisting evil actively is what all of the people in this volume share, but some have done so more directly than others. Yitzak Arad did so actively as a fighter against the Nazis; Marion Pritchard and Jan Karski as volunteers against the evil their co-citizens wreaked on Jews; Mordecai Paldiel's work is dedicated to proving that evil need not triumph over the human spirit. Whitney Harris can be seen as more concerned here with evil in the legal sense than in any religious context or psychological or philosophical way as he discusses the Nuremberg Trials. Dorothee Soelle speaks from a specifically theological point of view, Leo Eitinger the psychological (the ongoing impact of evil on the survivor). Emil Fackenheim's insights are philosophical, and Wiesel's are artistic/mystical.

To say more about each of these might be to becloud their own very clear words.

Perhaps a few words on the circumstances of each encounter will be in order (and they were *encounters*, not just "interviews" or "meetings"). First let me say that I have done a lot of interviewing in the thirty years I have been studying the Holocaust. In my television and radio experiences I had discussions with a wide variety of accomplished persons, from anthropologists and athletes to poets and the president of Mexico. Thus I had some background for attempting such a venture as this anthology of encounters. But as I reflect on the occasions of these dialogues, I am overwhelmed by the generosity of these good people to tell me about themselves, their activities, their ideas. I had not even met Marion Pritchard, Arnost Lustig, or Dorothee Soelle before interviewing them, yet their openness and great-heartedness were soon apparent.

I spoke with Lustig in his office at American University in Washington, D.C., in February 1986. I had known his son

Pepe when we were both associated with the United States Holocaust Memorial Council, and I had asked him if he thought that his father might be receptive to an interview. Apparently my work was not unknown to both of them, and the younger Lustig helped me arrange our meeting. I arrived at the campus early, as is my style—Lustig came late, as seems to be his style. Watching him interact with students was a great pleasure; he is quite popular and seems genuinely to enjoy their attention. It took us some time to get started on our interview, but we became instant friends and are now working on several projects together.

Simon Wiesenthal and I met for breakfast at a St. Louis hotel in the summer of 1988, and the tape of our interview is filled with clanging dishes, waiter interruptions, and laughter from other tables. This was probably our fourth meeting. I could have met Wiesenthal much sooner but chose not to because I was not interested in getting to know someone whose heart, I mistakenly thought, was filled with hatred. As a Nazi-hunter this *had* to be the case, I assumed. How wrong I was. There is a great distinction between revenge and the justice to which Wiesenthal is committed. He appears to me to be a man without rancor, one who does his job as thoroughly as the strictest Jewish laws regarding justice require, and is clearly an indefatigable worker filled with compassion for human suffering on every level.

The relationship with Yitzhak Arad was originally based upon my appointment to the International Advisory Board at Yad Vashem. I am one of only two Christians named to that body (the other being Franklin Littell, the father of all of us Christians engaged in Holocaust studies) and as such came to know Arad in his official capacity at meetings in Jerusalem or when I came to do research there. But our interview took place in Detroit, where we had both been invited to discuss a particular proposal involving the Holocaust Memorial Center in West Bloomfield, Michigan. This was in March 1988. Rabbi Charles Rozenzweig, who founded that truly model institution, had called the meeting, and I arranged to be in the car that picked up Dr. Arad at the airport. I taped our session in the back seat while traveling on Detroit expressways, which were not totally silent! Transcribing the recording was an interesting adventure all its own.

Mordecai Paldiel and I have encountered on three continents: in Jerusalem, in the United States, and in Oxford, England, where our dialogue took place in July of 1988. We were both speaking at the world conference Remembering for the Future, sponsored by the late Robert Maxwell, which brought together the greatest collection of Holocaust scholars from around the world ever assembled in one place. The weather was beautiful, and we did our talking while walking around one of the quadrangles at Oxford University. Paldiel's English is near perfect, his knowledge of his subject—those who helped to rescue Jews during the Holocaust—encyclopedic and at ready recall. He was the first person to earn a doctorate in Holocaust Studies in the United States (at Temple University).

The most difficult chapter in this book was the one with Jan Karski. We had met casually several times at various Holocaust commemorations in Philadelphia and Washington, D.C. He agreed to let me talk with him for this book in his Georgetown University office in September of 1985. It was a very moving experience for me, but somehow I could not get the chronology of events straight. We agreed that a second session was necessary. This was done in October of 1987 in his Maryland home. A third meeting was also required, again in his living room, and still, in my editing, I did not reflect his intentions properly. Not a young man, Dr. Karski felt he had given me enough of his energy and that future encounters might likewise prove ultimately futile. Nevertheless I persisted because his story is so important and inspiring and I found him to be deserving of a far better representation than I was giving him. I took the transcriptions of the three recordings, matched them with certain lectures Karski had given and with articles by and about him, as well as his book *Story of a Secret State*, and was able to "compile," as it were, the interview that appears here. Karski, the epitome of the tall, lean, graceful, disciplined, courteous diplomat, was patient and helpful throughout what must have been at least a minor ordeal for him.

Vermont, where she now lives, was the locale of my first visit with Marion Pritchard in October 1987. I had been so impressed by her story as she told it in the film *The Courage to Care* (and in the book of the same title by Carol Rittner and Sondra Myers) that I wanted very much to meet and record her. She and her husband Anton met me at a New Hampshire airport and drove me to her office just across the state border, where we spent several hours talking. It is difficult to describe the humility of this good person. I think some of this quality is evident in her words contained in this volume.

Leon Wells and I had been at least acquaintances for several years before the interview with him took place. I had particularly admired his independent judgments on certain Holocaust issues, especially on the failure of some Jewish organizations in America to come fully to the aid of Jews fleeing Nazi persecution in Europe. Wells's book *Who Speaks for the Vanquished?* documents his charges on this topic and had just been published when we met again in March of 1988 at Kent State University, where we were both speakers at an annual Holocaust conference.

Whitney Harris is a St. Louis treasure. He and his wife Jane have contributed enormously to the culture of our city, and both are widely respected. What appears in these pages is an edited transcript of two half-hour television interviews I did with him in July 1986 for a sixteen-part series I produced with Jerry Rock directing, titled *The Holocaust: Can It Happen Again?* I might mention that the transcription hardly needed editing. Harris is one of those people who speaks so eloquently that, unlike most of us, even his ordinary speech is rendered in impeccable English and in complete sentences.

Leo Eitinger is the most modest of men. A person of vast achievement, he is soft-spoken, self-effacing, and a great joy to know. I have a copy of his text for an autobiography, which I am sorry to say may never be published because he is so unassuming that what is in reality a very exciting and important life is "too humbly" told. He has been repeatedly recognized for his very valuable contributions in the field of psychiatry, but perhaps his major accomplishment occurred when, in his capacity as a medical doctor, he helped to operate on a boy in Auschwitz and saved his life. That child was Elie Wiesel. While I have conversed with Eitinger in his city of Oslo, in St. Louis, in Oxford, and elsewhere, our interview actually took place at the Waldorf-Astoria Hotel in New York, where we were both participating in a Holocaust gathering in March of 1982.

Dorothee Soelle is a German Protestant feminist theologian who gives honor to all four of those terms. She seems to understand the Jewish Jesus in ways that many others do not. Her insights into failure of German Christianity during the Hitler period are enlightening; Soelle's meditations on the situation of women in contemporary society and her feminist approach to theology are beacons lighting the way for many of us. We first met when she came to speak at my school, Webster University, and she permitted me an interview. She came again in February 1982 when I organized a sixtieth birthday commemoration for Elie Wiesel (along with a host of other major Holocaust figures), and on both occasions proved that she was not only a profound writer but an impressive speaker as well.

The soft-spoken Emil Fackenheim and I met one morning in November of 1987 in his hotel room in St. Louis to produce what is here published. Fackenheim is an early morning person who appears to adjust almost immediately to international time zone changes. No matter where he is, apparently, he prefers breakfast at 6:00 AM; our interview began about a half-hour after that. We had first met in 1976 in New York State at a conference on Elie Wiesel and the Holocaust Universe where forty invited persons met for three days. Like the others gathered, I was so impressed by Fackenheim that I made a mental note to prepare myself to interview him one day.

Over the years I have had the privilege of interviewing Elie Wiesel in many locales: New York, California, England, Missouri. The interview done specifically for this book took place in his New York City apartment in June of 1991. As I mentioned earlier, our first encounter was on *Continuum*, a half-hour television program. Later interviews appeared in such periodicals as *Jubilee, Commonweal,* and *Holocaust and Genocide Studies.* We have cooperated on many other projects over the eighteen years I have known Wiesel. He has always been warm, helpful, instructive, and inspiring.

This volume, then, is the culmination of a great deal of cooperation, combined with, for me, deep, deep appreciation. It has been an honor to prepare the texts.

ARNOST LUSTIG

Arnost Lustig's books and stories have been translated into more than twenty languages, including Polish, German, Japanese, Hindi, Yiddish, Esperanto, and French. His best known fiction deals with the Holocaust experience of children. He himself survived the Holocaust as a boy.

Born in Prague, Lustig came to the United States after having a distinguished career in writing and cinema in Czechoslovakia. He was a lecturer in film and literature at universities in his home country as well as in Japan, Canada, Israel, and the United States. His novel *A Prayer for Katerina Horovitzova* (1974) was nominated for the National Book Award, and the television adaptation of that work received nine international prizes. Additionally, he has garnered a number of awards for radio scripts and stories in Czechoslovakia, Australia, and the United States. Among his works are *Dita Saxova* (1962); his "Children of the Holocaust" series (1977), including *Darkness Casts No Shadow, Night and Hope,* and *Diamonds in the Night; The Unloved* (1985); and *Indecent Dreams* (1988). Lustig was a war correspondent during the Arab-Israeli conflict (1948-1949) and served as a correspondent for Czechoslovak Radio in Europe, Asia, and North America. He later taught at the University of Iowa's International Writers Program, then at Drake University, and in 1973 he began a long teaching career at American University.

HJC You said in one of your books that you simply want to kill as long as you will be killed. You say you want to drink justice, but you talk about the line between justice and revenge as being a very thin line, since everything around us teaches us to kill. I'm wondering whether in some way you are killing when you write.

AL First, I must tell you that I never killed anyone and I'm very happy for that. I believe that I can be a writer only because I never killed and because I don't intend to kill. I have a technique when I write that suggests and makes the reader come to his own conclusions—but I *wish* him to make a certain conclusion. So when I say that my philosophy of writing is either to be killed or to kill, I mean that I would like to make the reader feel that I hate both, that I hate to be killed and I hate to kill. I'm asking, "What should we do to change the world?" But I don't express this question explicitly because that wouldn't be writing. That would be a textbook of philosophy.

HJC So many writers (like Camus, Sartre, or Fuentes) have said that, particularly since the end of the Second World War, either you're on the side of the victims or you're on the side of the executioners. You have to choose one or the other.

AL I cannot accept this choice, and this is what I am writing about. I am writing about the possibility of changing the human condition so that my children won't have that question put before them: to kill or not to kill. You know, sometimes everything makes you feel that you are very close to being an enigma. Let us say that you are a fish. You were born to swim near the surface. But at once some unknown pressure you are not used to pushes you down almost flat to the very bottom of the sea, where there are dark waters, and you lose your orientation because you were used to other waters without pressure. Or you are a fish down there used to the dark waters and you come up and see something completely different. This is what happened to the Jews. They were fish swimming in completely different waters than those they were thrown into and asked to swim in. They couldn't swim, they couldn't orient themselves.

I was in three camps, in the fortress in Theresienstadt, Buchenwald, and Auschwitz-Birkenau; and I was extremely lucky that I survived. I know that everybody who survived lives only because someone else died. Many times I wished to die, not to see what I saw. And I was not in the worst of conditions. I didn't have to kill anyone, to eat human flesh, to humiliate anyone. I think that there were many times when I was really mad, not completely responsible for myself but maybe, even then, lucky.

HJC   For instance?

AL   When they killed my father, who was a beautiful man, who never did anyone any wrong; I was singing a song which I had sung a few days ago with my father, for we saw that in a clandestine cabaret. It was from *Die Fledermaus*, and it had a line, "Happy is the man who forgets what cannot be changed." I couldn't comprehend what happened. I was seventeen years old. I was coming from the world where good was rewarded and evil punished. I was standing there at the poles with wires under high voltage, under cloudy skies, singing for an hour or two, and I refused to go back to the barracks because I didn't care for life. Thirty yards away or so were the gas chambers. Flames were coming out from the chimneys. Fortunately there were friends with me. All my life I was extremely lucky with friends. They dragged me back into the barracks because after dark I would have been shot. I remember that many times in Auschwitz-Birkenau I wished for an air-raid by the Americans or Russians or British, not just for the destruction of Auschwitz-Birkenau but also for my own destruction. I was young, without much education, except for this experience, and I must have been lucky because somebody always helped me.

I remember in Auschwitz-Birkenau one day in October 1944. I was freezing. Some man, around forty, told me, "Boy, you are freezing, come among us." I said to myself, "My God, these people are laughing at me. They are freezing themselves." I didn't pay attention. They told me, "Come in." And they took me, put me in the middle, pressed me for five minutes with their own bodies because they didn't have anything else. They warmed me up and told me, "Now run." This made me happy. It was a human touch you can dream about. Once you get such a lesson about friendship and solidarity, you know that friendship and solidarity exist. Finally, I escaped the camp, after six days of starving, from a death transport for Buchenwald, Dachau, or to Theresienstadt. I am not certain about the destination. (I didn't wait to find out for sure.) If it had been going to Dachau, we would definitely have died. In Theresienstadt, maybe. I escaped and lived illegally in Prague and took part in the anti-Nazi uprising during the last five days of the war. My assignment was to cross Paris avenue under the German machine-gun tower and bring food from an apartment to the hospital where I was hiding. My mother and my sister survived. But I cannot forget those moments of truth when the best people were dying and the worst were only postponing their deaths for an hour, a day, two days, two nights. Sometimes for an unbearable price.

I know that man is extremely close to the enemy sometimes. At the same time, I saw many good people, many brave people, many clever or wise or unselfish people. I know that change is possible. For better or for worse. I am interested in the possibility of a change in man for the better. I wrote about these things in what I consider my best book, *Diamonds of the Night*. And, of course, in my thirteen other books. And I am not finished. I put all that is good or better or around me into them.

The first day after the war, I looked at thousands of German soldiers in Prague marching in captivity. They were beaten by the revolutionary guards and some jumped into the icy river. I had a chance to kill as many of them as I could wish. I had a brief discussion with a liberating soldier who offered me his machine gun to feel free to do whatever my heart wished. I told him I was sick of death. I was sick of beating, of injustice. To be in love with death would bring you close to the Nazis. They were in love with death. Death was everything for them—life nothing. As one Czech writer said, death was their best friend. I was quite satisfied to see that the Germans under the same pressure behaved just as the Jews did. Or the French. The English. The Americans. The Russians. The Czechs. All people are equal. In all ways. I learned that lesson the hard way. It did not make me happy. It was not a merry recognition. But such is life. It only confirmed that man can be good, bad, very good, very bad. Sometimes both. And a thousand shades in between. One for one second, and another for the next. This is what I saw in my life in the camps and immediately after them.

You know, I am writing about camps like Jack London was writing about the Gold Rush, or Joseph Conrad about the people and seas, and Isaac Babel about people smashed by the revolution. What's in your blood, you heart, your brain. You can write only about what you know, feel, live. I was born into it and I am still fascinated by it because it was such a treasure of human experience that if it hadn't been paid with such havoc, like the death of your father and the death of the best people you knew, I would say that it was the best schooling I could have gotten. (I hope you understand the metaphor.)

Now, the problem is what am I going to do with it, number one. Number two, if I stick with it, will it darken my horizons about what is going on in the world now? The world didn't stop. I was a reporter traveling throughout the world, so I know a little. I was in Cambodia, which was a beautiful kingdom. They killed a million—two or three million people. It's impossible to count. Then I was in India and China. I saw in Calcutta human conditions to compare with what I saw in the camps—you cannot make comparison to Auschwitz-Birkenau—and yet you can compare human conditions. You can, if you know what hunger is, and how hunger diminishes and humiliates you. Hunger, anxiety, fear, cold, insecurity, illnesses, hopelessness, the desperation of children without mothers and fathers, sisters without brothers, men without women and women without men. And I know that

Auschwitz-Birkenau and these other camps didn't come from nowhere. There must have been something in the air already and it didn't disappear afterwards. The most ashamed I ever was of my own country, Czechoslovakia, and its conqueror, Russia, was when I discovered that long after World War II they had concentration camps, that the idea of socialism went from utopia to murder. So I asked the questions, "And what to do with it? How to behave?"

HJC   How do you reflect this in your writing and teaching?

AL   I say to my students today, "Why do I teach you the Jewish catastrophe?" I don't like teaching it, believe me, but I say to myself, "Okay, someone has to do it." It's not pleasant; I could be teaching how to write a screenplay, how to write a story. I could be teaching European literature, short stories, world literature. But I'm teaching the Jewish catastrophe (next to the rest), and I tell them, "Look, there's only one reason, and you should learn it. To be stronger, not for tears. To be more clever. To share an experience dearly paid for by the death of grandfathers and grandmothers and uncles and aunts you could never see. So that you know what happened, that people can be as beautiful as Anne Frank or Janusz Korczak were, and as ugly as Adolf Hitler or Reinhardt Heydrich and Heinrich Himmler. That this can happen to you. I teach you so that in case it happens to you, you will not be weak or desperately trustful like the generation of Jews who did not believe it because they were completely unprepared, because they were too civilized and forgot or suppressed their instinct for survival and had many other shortcomings. You will know enough and be ready to say, 'No, I'm not going. I know what Buchenwald was, I know what Auschwitz-Birkenau was. I will defend myself. I will fight.'" This is why I teach. And now you have to add what I have learned afterwards. I think that there is a necessity to see.

HJC   How is it connected with your writing and your being a writer?

AL   First of all, being a writer is the only thing which gives me a wonderful feeling of beauty and meaning, and, of course, some stability. Let me say that only a few other things leave me with such a feeling. But nobody can write about what's not really in him, and this period which I don't like to call "Holocaust" is inside of me. (I don't like it because Holocaust is made up of two Greek words: "destroyed by fire." This is what happened in ancient Greece, an earthquake or by great fire. Jews were burned by fire, in the end, but only after being humiliated and killed by German Nazis and their collaborators of almost all nations in Europe.) Call it a Jewish catastrophe, a man-made catastrophe which can happen again, perhaps not only to Jews. It must be studied as objectively as possible to help make man stronger. It is in the air. So, I teach about it and write about it as a most profound human experience.

HJC Are you well known enough?

AL You asked me already why these books are not as widely read as they deserve to be. What do you mean, exactly? I think that to write about this Jewish catastrophe and to search for fame at the same time is almost indecent. I'm really content as it is. It's not entertaining reading, despite my attempts to make it the best that I can. I'm not going to judge it. It's up to the reader. It is a difficult experience because if I hadn't been in the camps and somebody invited me to see one, two, three, four films or let me read too many books about this, I don't know how I would react. I'm not pushing my books too much. I'm happy that they are published. There are editions in English, Japanese, Estonian, Norwegian, Spanish, and German so the best stories are slowly becoming known. I think that my time will come, let us say five, fifty years from today when children from a new generation will be trying to get a picture of what happened. Like today, let us say, we are getting the real picture of Napoleon. Only now, forty-five years after the war, I think it is the duty of all writers who were there to write about it as well as they can. Not to be concerned if they are known or famous or well paid. A good and honest writer will always survive, somehow. This I learned in my writing life, and I am now sixty-three years old. History will select which writers are important for the future. You can't select yourself. We really don't know. It's a relay. . . . Or a mosaic. We can only contribute with our books.

I know that this generation is at the end. Maybe it will be some inspiration for much fiction. I don't know how much. After all, Tolstoy did not experience the Napoleonic war and wrote by far the best book on it without having been there. It's nonsense to claim that a fiction about Belsen is either not a fiction or not about Belsen. I know that there are certain things about which those who were there feel strongly, but those who were there also are handicapped. They do not lie, but can they reveal the full amount of truth? The full amount of humiliation? Who has a stomach for that? I was telling my son today, "The greatest crime of the Nazis was that they killed the Jews: you have only one life, you cannot get your life back. But the very next crime—which was almost as bad as the killing—was that they humiliated Jews before they killed them. They wanted them to accept that they are inferior before dying. This humiliation was so enormous that the mechanism of the mind, even a first-class mind, or the most open, sincere, almost cynical mind, must suppress this humiliation *somehow."* Did you read Frankl? Bettelheim? There you have it like an open palm. They testify that this is the core of our problems. This sum of humiliation will never be discovered: Jewish writers—including these two—are unable to overcome the sum of this humiliation because it drowns them. And non-Jewish writers who did overcome it partly, like Tadeusz Borowski, who wrote a most Jewish book really, tell most of it. He commited suicide—he gassed himself. Paul Celan killed himself. Piotr Ravitz, Jean Amery, Primo Levi—all killed themselves. After the war. Liberated. Rehabilitated. Free. Free? That horrible humiliation tied their hands.

It's impossible to communicate the humiliation. It kills. The humiliation of the killed and of the survivors plus the impossibility of transcribing it forcefully enough. There is no writer who can tell it all. Who can take it all. You know, if a rabbi were asked to eat his own excrement, let us say, in front

of his own son and was told that if he did not, his child would
be shot, he would do it. People were eating their own flesh,
brains, drinking blood, there is no end to it. Can you write
about such things? Yes—maybe. How? The whole picture?
An understatement? By indirection? This is only a mild
example that I'm giving you. Humiliation of fathers in front
of children, children in front of fathers, mothers, sisters,
members of families betraying each other, sometimes killing
each other. Sure, there are examples of the most splendid
heroism of others, in the same conditions. So I think of that
great crime of the Nazis—the humiliation of Jews. It will
never be forgotten, never forgiven, but also never described,
never discredited. I can tell you that I saw ugly examples of it.
But what I saw is only a splinter, anyway.

HJC What do your students say?

AL My students say it's unbelievable. I ask, "What do
you say is unbelievable? Try to imagine: I wouldn't feed you
for three weeks. I wouldn't let you go to the restroom. You
would stay locked in a room without windows. I can tell you
that in three weeks you would become cannibals, animals."
The problem of civilization is that civilization is growing
slowly, millimeter by millimeter, and the tiny crust of it can
be scratched in a week, a month, a few years. My idea is that
the best writer should contribute to the civilization, at least a
millimeter; to scratch this tiny surface of civilization is so
easy. I saw it.

I have a friend here in America who was a cannibal in a
camp near to Auschwitz. He ate the flesh of the dead bodies
of his friends because they hadn't fed him for three weeks.
They were mad. I knew a rabbi who stole bread. (In my
number 21 in the Gypsy camp.) But he was not a rabbi any
more; he was a madman who was hungry, just like my cannibal friend. This man who ate humans saved also his little
sister in the camps. He was not even a full Jew, only partly;
his father was so poor that he sent him to the Jewish or-
phanage before the war. They didn't look Jewish at all. But
they know what is Jewish fate. They shared it with us. He
was later an Israeli paratrooper and now he is living here—

very well. He's over sixty. He would never tell you. That is the duty of the best of the writers. To tell, and to tell it well. To serve, to make the world more human. To speak the truth. It's a wonderful service. The truth is sometimes ugly. But what to do? How to express even the ugly beautifully? I think it is necessary to see in perspective, not to make it a biological survey like about dead butterflies. Not to make it a museum which is useful to the future but which is only a part of many other things.

HJC   Can you compare yourself to some other writers?

AL   I am not comparing myself in some way to anybody. And at the same time, we're all in the same boat. All serious writers. You know, there is no one writer who can say it all. As I said, it can only be a mosaic, a panorama. If somebody thinks he is as great as Mount Everest, he is wrong, even if he gets all the prizes on the globe.

I will tell you a story. I was once sent to the Himalayas, and I wanted to see Mount Everest, close up, of course. There were people there who had spent six weeks waiting for the clouds to go away. It was very crowded. Somehow I was lucky and I saw Mount Everest on my second morning. I was disappointed. The sisters of Mount Everest were so tall that the mountain did not look like the tallest on earth. But still, it was the highest; it just didn't look so. And so it is with writers, with all writers, including the authors about the Jewish catastrophe. No one can be the only one.

And this is why I'm sometimes sorry that in America they are looking for the frontrunner; it's hard because America loves an extreme. Americans are sometimes satisfied with just one. It's a fashion label, almost.

HJC   Are you complaining?

AL   I'm not complaining about myself. I'm a relatively lucky one. I have had seven books in thirteen or fourteen editions published in fifteen years. And, what's also good, new books ready to publish after they will be translated. (That's my problem, I have to pay for a translator more than I get in honoraria.) It's only a matter of translation, and I'm not in a hurry—because there is no hurry. They are written anyway. But there are so many good writers in Europe and around the world, and nobody knows them. Piotr Rawicz, for example, wrote one of the very, very best books ever written about the Jewish catastrophe. Once published, hard cover, it disappeared. Chaim Guri, too, (*The Chocolate Deal*), Kasimir Brandys, also more of Tadeusz Borowski—never published in this country. Rudnicky—I think that we are only shadows of this man and not just because he spent those years on the other side in Warsaw during the Jewish uprising. Experts know him, but readers? or the Jewish public? No. I would like to teach those writers. But their books are not reprinted. There is no *one* writer. It can only be a group of writers.

HJC Just parenthetically, is Rudnicky Jewish? I don't think he is.

AL He is—at least partly—but it doesn't matter. I tell you, I wish that more non-Jews would write about it because Jews are embarrassed about the level of their own humiliation, as I said. I'm not going to describe my father when he saw us going and he couldn't do anything. I am not going into the consciousness of my parents. You can do it poetically, but sometimes poetry is not enough. On the other hand, as Aristotle said, if you have a choice between history and poetry, poetry will take you farther. And if you have a dynamo of your own experience plus poetry, it can get you pretty far. But then you are scared of what you are standing in front of and how to describe it. How? You wish not to know what you know, not to see, not to feel, and yet. . . .

HJC You have chosen to concentrate most of your efforts on what happened to young people. Why?

AL Because I was young.

HJC Which approach do you choose as a man who writes? Are you sure you are not on a wrong path?

AL I told you first of all that I feel like a writer, and maybe my mind has this, not synchronization, but simply—after all those years—the way of a writer's mind. So I really need to feel that what I am writing is the truth, that I am not a liar. Of course, an error or a mistake in conception is not a lie. But it ruins your piece. So I need to feel absolutely faithful to

the reality of truth. No deviations, not even one degree. I
must know that every line I write, if I were to die tomorrow,
was the truth and as the truth, will stay, not waiting for me to
say, "Sorry, it was not exact and I would like to correct it." So
I'm writing everything as if I were going to die tomorrow.
Every honest writer does it. It's a writer's approach. I have to
cover myself like a radius of sun. Where my sun goes, there is
the life of my literature. I can cover only what I really feel.
That is my sun.

HJC Let us go back. Why young people? Why the very old
next? But seldom the middle aged.

AL Young people? Because I was young. Or old people?
Because I felt terribly sorry for all the old people. And I know
that we survived in Theresienstadt because the Jewish leadership—the Zionists—took food from the old people and fed
it to the young out of a human and idealistic belief that it's
the future generation that will build Eretz Israel (the promised land) just as Communists believed only the young will
lead the future revolution. It was wrong but understandable. I
am one of those who survived maybe because of that approach. I am only trying to tell the truth. And it covers young
people and old people. I am not yet finished.

HJC Young people symbolize hope for you?

AL Old people symbolize hope, too, you know. Hope is
not a property of age. There is one problem sometimes, that
my approach is not so idealistic as it is factual. I'm trying to
say what I felt, what I saw. And because it's poetry, I have a
license for it. Hope is one of the greatest dimensions of men
in spite of the fact that hopelessness can bring you closer to
your own defense. If I die, so, the enemy will die with me. It's
nothing new. Take Samson. But hope is like a hidden sun. You
feel some sparks or some warmth in the cold, and it makes
you stronger. It's like being in love, it's invisible. It's invisible, but it's strong. It can be a passion. There were people
who, if they had said to themselves, "Now I will drop dead,"
would indeed have done so. They were already dead people,
corpses, but if they had hope, then you saw corpses walking
around and you knew there is only one power. Nobody can

explain it, only people who believe in God. But if you don't
believe in God, let us say, how can you explain these people's
hope? Hope is really beautiful. They can take everything
from you but hope. Except if they kill you. And I think that
later the Nazis were so angry that they killed hope together
with the people, faster and faster. They killed everything. Or
so they believed. I have to go back to it so that if I am writing
about this time of catastrophe, about young people, I want an
American boy, or a Czech boy, or a French boy, to feel that it's
about him. That he could have been Anne Frank, that he
could have been me. He's lucky he was not, but who knows
for how long he will be safe? My father also didn't believe
that he had proof that man can come so far or so deep.

I think that if there hadn't been Jews, the Nazis would
have found a different group. They needed someone like the
Jews. The Jews were comfortable for them for several reasons: they were a minority; often they looked different; they
were strangers; and they were a people of strong morality.
The Nazis wanted to destroy the morality which built this
civilization. Hitler hated the Romans, he hated Christianity,
and he hated Judaism. He said those were three ideologies
which didn't solve anything. There were fifty-five million
unemployed people in Europe when Hitler took over Germany. He wanted to go back to a time before those three
ideologies. But of those three ideologies, the most dangerous
for him was Moses' Jewish concept of law, which came to the
conclusion that you cannot build a civilization without three
simple concepts. Concept number one: the ability to recognize good and bad, right and wrong, just and unjust. Everybody understands, everybody can identify with that. If Hitler
had been able to destroy this concept, then good would be
defined as that which serves Germany. He needed to destroy
this concept in order to make his people feel that killing Jews
was not a crime. If you feel that killing is not a crime, you
have no remorse. He also said that the human conscience was
a Jewish invention that cripples the mind of man, just like
circumcision cripples his body. I don't think that in the
beginning they wanted to destroy European Jewry, but later

they came to the conclusion that they must do so—that they could do so—that the world would accept it and that future generations would praise them. They were partly wrong, partly right. We cannot judge how wrong they were.

HJC   Isn't it demonic?

AL   To see Nazis, Germans, as demons is nonsense. They were very human. They had a lot of humanistic concepts but they were wrong. I am trying to write from a universal perspective. I was a human creature, born as a Czech Jew, and because of fate I was a part of something I would have liked to avoid—but nobody could. And now I am writing about it as a hidden and obvious experience.

HJC   You present Germans as humans, too. You don't present them as completely evil, nor do you present the Jews in the camps as completely good.

AL   If there hadn't been good Germans, I wouldn't be sitting here today. I knew a man, my boss in the factory (I don't know if he had been as nice two years before at the time of Hitler's victories) who lost three children and he told me that I was like his son, and he brought me food every day, not only for myself but also for my friends. And there was an S.S. whom I told I would help after the war if he would help me here and now, and he brought me food. After the war, I met a friend who spent a year in prison because he had helped a German family, bringing them food from Czechoslovakia over the border when they were hungry, because they had helped him. So I think it's a mistake to see Germans as demons because that would be too easy. They were human beings. They had many goals similar to everybody else's. They wanted what was best for Germany. So they stole from Jews, Russians, Czechs, Communists, Social Democrats, Jehovah's Witnesses. They took everything from everyone in order to make Germany strong. Because they felt pressures of space, they wanted to liquidate 150 million people in the East to make Germany great and comfortable. Every emperor wants to make his empire bigger, greater, better. Everything they wanted was a human desire. For them it's not a matter of right or wrong, justice or injustice. What serves Germany was

seen as being right for Germany. They killed 66,000 of their
own soldiers in Buchenwald, in a horrible way for which I, as
a Jew, felt sorry. This same thing could happen to the French,
to the Americans, tomorrow. It happened in the Soviet empire. So I am trying to find out.

HJC   What are your conclusions?

AL   I think that something was missing from them. Man,
who created himself from an animal, adds something to this
personality every civilized day. We cannot take this something in hand. It's intangible. We cannot see it. We cannot
hear it. But it is just like hope, which makes you somebody
else. I think that all those invisible concepts of what's possible for a human being to achieve, under certain circumstances, makes him heavier. I mean heavier mentally. This
Nazi movement, because it was not a movement of one but a
movement of all, of many, stripped the individual of something, made him miss something—let us say respect for man,
for every man, same and different, as fingerprints are, to
make it very simple. The dignity one man feels, not the blind
pride of a crowd. If you don't feel any respect for any other
person, because you are bitter or because of your nature or
for whatever reason, then something is missing from you. I
am trying to find out what it was that those people had
missing. Perhaps they thought that it was only temporary,
that they would kill Jews, no big deal, and then start anew,
washing their hands, with Jewish gold and Jewish posses-
sions, houses, jobs. The killing, then, seemed not so bad, just
unpleasant. Let us forget yesterday today and today tomorrow. Materially, it was good for Germany. But there were
many Germans killed, too.

I met beautiful German prisoners in camp. To forget this
would be a crime. And I will never forget it. But again, there is
a duty to see it in the right proportion, not to forget for good
the bad and not to forget for bad the good. To see how it really
was, not to seek revenge. Now we have lived forty years in
peace. Justice, after forty years of peace, is like a flower. You
cannot water it with hate. You cannot keep hate for forty
years if you are an ordinary man. Maybe if you are a sadist or a

masochist or a pervert. But if you are normal, and we are not
going to discuss what's normal, if you are a decent man, you
know that revenge won't make you happy. Revenge is not
justice. Justice must be pure. But as a writer, you have to
know what is revenge and what is justice, how to describe
each. Where they touch each other. If people feel that there is
justice in revenge, then I have to write about it. If they feel
that there is revenge in their justice, then I should write
about that too. I am a judge only indirectly. The reader is the
judge. I'm only an observer of a sort, an honest observer,
taking part. Some Germans were good. Thank God for them.
I wish that they would multiply by the million, because then
I would know that if another Nazi were to come, they would
say stop, shut up, go away. I don't know how objective I am,
though I try to be.

HJC   You mentioned the humiliation aspect of the concentration camp experience. One of the things that I see in
your work is a number of your characters striving to maintain their dignity in the face of all that humiliation.

AL   Dignity, maybe, is the same as hope. For me, it is a
basic, most important virtue. Sometimes, to walk tall in
camp gave you something because they wanted you to bow, to
feel how small you really were. Dignity is a beautiful human
trait. It is a creation of men, of civilization, of ten thousand
years. They can take your life, but it's very hard to take your
dignity. It's just like with hope and other human virtues. To
be honest is to be beautiful. It can be also stupid, but it's
always beautiful. A man who was honest in camp was a saint.
It is so easy to steal when you are hungry because we are all
creators of our own morality. We all know about situation
ethics. What's necessary is right. We are all our own Moseses.
Or Christs. Or Buddhas. If you don't believe that God gave
you those rules of morality, then you have to accept that
everybody creates his own morality. And what's moral and
immoral is decided by each person, sometimes selfishly,
sometimes wrongly, but it makes sense to each individual.
Maybe it's a situation morality and always was. I don't know.
It's not what's written in the laws. I saw many laws which

lacked justice. I saw people following what was legal but wrong and what was illegal but right, given the circumstances. I saw people who were permitted to steal because they were hungry, and they never did. They were really like saints. It sounds strange, but I am in love with those people, even those dead for forty-five years now, because I knew they represented a triumph for humanity. But nobody knows about them. So this is also one of my motives for writing these stories.

Writers have discussed for years the fourth dimension of writing. There are—according to Hemingway—three dimensions in writing: the present, which is the action; the past, which is the motives for the action; and the future, which is the impact of the action. But there is a fourth dimension. Hemingway, for instance, talks a lot about this dimension without ever explaining what it is. Perhaps it's a soul. I think it's a soul of man incorporated in one's writing, and if you are able to breathe the soul into your fictional protagonist, then you have this fourth dimension. People can take literature, which is only paper and written words, not miracles, as if it were flesh and blood—but writers have to. A story must have a soul, its own soul. The soul of men. I believe that you can get this fourth dimension only if you are absolutely honest plus lucky. If you really believe that, in the moment of writing, you are like these people who didn't steal when they could have. It doesn't mean that is impossible for you to stop writing and go to a restaurant for a beer—or get drunk as a dog. But when you write you can sometimes reach this fourth dimension.

HJC   You said something in these last remarks that harkens back to what I thought about when I asked my first question, "What do you kill when you write?" In a certain sense, you're killing their death, aren't you?

AL   You cannot kill death, but you can protest it passionately. It's like when somebody dies to you. My father died and I couldn't accept his death because there was no grave and he was killed under such humiliation, because he had no idea what was going on in those gas chambers where people were scratching their eyes and biting their noses, where there was excrement and blood. It was a horrible picture and everybody was part of this picture. Children were stepped on as the strong climbed to reach the ceiling to get the last breath of air. So I never went to the cemetery, in spite of my mother, who had his name engraved on the stone of his father and mother. It was a blind protest. I knew that I was wrong, but I objected to this kind of death. So I didn't accept it. But after years I came to the conclusion that I couldn't change the fact of his death with my protests. My objections were primitive. I wanted at least to keep the name of my father. So to write about those dead is really for me a poor, a weak triumph of life, but it is a triumph nonetheless. Very humble, very modest, very personal.

You know, we all try to reach for some immortality. It's an illusion of man: the worker who says on a Sunday stroll to his child, "This is the house I worked on, that piece of wall, these are the bricks I lay." It's a piece of immortality at least, and I understand it and I love it. Writing about these people is like this mason telling his child to look at the house. I'm saying, "Look, they were people who did not even have graves, who died like animals, worse than animals, who were killed for doing nothing, only to be robbed of everything—materially, mentally, physically." When I write, I am a different person. I have a good nature and I am carefree. When I write, it gives me a sense of responsibility which pulls me. I am never so responsible as when I am writing. Don't ask me why. I don't know why. I could tell it, but now that I am in my sixties, I will tell *you* all my secrets. It includes what I can't explain but what I feel and what exists. I really don't do interviews of this sort, but we have struck a chord and there is nothing to hide any more.

HJC Somebody once asked Hemingway what he meant by his latest novel and he said, "How do I know, I only wrote it." You sound like there's a little of that element in you. When you're writing, you don't know what gets a hold of you.

AL No, no! You know, you dream you want, you desire. And your desire is a composition of material things. Maybe

more. Writing is magic. You are a writer, too, so you know
that you have a feeling like when you make love. And as if
dying. Silence. Peace. The end as a meaning of all things.
Maybe even when you are dying and it's brief, when you are
lucky. But when you write, you are in a trance for an afternoon, an evening, a nighttime, a week, a month, or with
interruptions for a year, and it's beautiful. So you do it also for
selfish reasons. I would like to say that not everything I am
describing here is so unselfish. I'm simply doing it because it
would be hard for me not to do it. You can ask writers why
they write, and you will get a very similar answer in spite of a
thousand differences that they have.

I had a great life in Prague, in Bohemia, as a writer and
film-maker. If I had wanted to see Honolulu in better years,
they would have sent me to Honolulu twice. If I said I wanted
to visit San Francisco, to see the shore, the house and the
grave of Jack London, I went. But if I had stayed in Prague, I
wouldn't have been able to be a writer anymore. So I decided
to give up everything except being a writer. Old Jews believed
that honesty—to be moral—is like a bird flying over the
ocean. You can never stop moving your wings, otherwise you
would drown. It cannot be inherited. You have to conquer it
every day again. So, you see, wings, freedom. And it makes
me happy. ("Happy" is a stupid word. You have to excuse me.)
This is the selfish part of it. It's such a satisfaction to start and
finish a sentence, a story, a book. You know exactly if the
sentence, [the] story, the book is good or wrong. If it's not
good, you let many people read it and you ask their opinions
and help. When it's good, you don't show it to anyone—you
know it's good and that's it.

HJC How is it that so many Holocaust writers (I'm talking about male writers now) do not create good female characters, yet you have Dita Saxova and Katerina Horovitzova
and Pearla and others? How are they possible?

AL I tell you. I had a beautiful mother, really a beautiful
woman. A working woman and a very good woman. In my
life, the best things I got were from women. I was in camps
with women. We were 2,000 Jews from Bohemia, 2,000 Pol-

ish Catholic women from Warsaw, from the uprising in 1944—they were beaten ten times more than I was because they sang Catholic songs for Christmas—and 2,000 Italian deserters, who were forbidden under the sentence of death to make love to German women while their husbands and brothers and lovers were fighting for the Reich. Yet they did it every day.

I will tell you a story which I just finished for the book *Street of Lost Brothers*. In Auschwitz-Birkenau I waited every day to hear at night the singing from the women's camp. When they sent mothers or daughters into the gas chambers the rest sang for those who remained, to comfort them. And finally those for whom they sang joined in and then they all sang the entire night. I knew they sang only when someone was being killed. There was an uprising in crematorium #4 in October of 1944 and women were smuggling things for it. It is a pleasure for me to write about women. Why? Because I'm excited, actually, about women. They teach me the deepest mystery of man. I wish to know what this mystery is. Nobody knows, not even women themselves.

HJC   You've had the good fortune to be creative in several media. You said something earlier about writing meaning so much to you. What about filmmaking?

AL   It's a pleasure. (It brings you money, that's the main difference.) Writing is for reflection, inner vision; film is for the eye, as others have said. This strange liquid called fame which ever parades so fast. I do it still. Maybe we will make a film with a Czech director in New York, *The Unloved*. The contract is signed. For Pepe, my son, and his director, I wrote the screenplay *Precious Legacy*, for which I shared an Emmy with two other screenwriters. It was shown on 360 stations from coast to coast. Four films, based on my stories and my screenplays, *Diamonds of the Night*, *Transport from Paradise*, *Dita Saxova*, and *A Bit to Eat*, were just bought by Facet Video Company in Chicago, one of the biggest in America. I became part of the film industry because in Europe, if you have best-selling books, they employ you as a screenwriter. They pay you for existing, and if you write a screenplay they pay you extra. So nobody would say no to writing for film. But if somebody were to ask me, "Film or books?" I would say books. Books take you everywhere. Books are the mothers of everything. Books are the mother of film, too. I like filmmaking. I was employed for ten years in the studio. I made two hour-long documentaries, one for ABC, *Stolen Childhood*, and one for Italian TV, and *Katerina Horovitzova* was made into a beautiful TV film and confiscated forever in Prague. It won eight first prizes all over the world. Elia Kazan was in Prague and saw *Diamonds of the Night* and *Transport from Paradise*. He said, "You would never have gotten money for such a film in America."

I was invited to the International Writing Program in Iowa City through the recommendation of George Stevens from the American Film Institute because he saw films based on my screenplays in Prague. It could have taken me to Hollywood. Only I felt that it was not good to go to Hollywood with my children unprepared. Lots of drugs and so on—not my world. I needed some place quiet to look around and to see what I was going to do. And I was quite lucky, again. I got a teaching position at the American University in Washington, D.C. Now I teach. This is also connected with writing. And I get to spend all day with young people. That's worth gold. You feel for whom you are writing. You see your readers.

HJC What influence did your journalism experience have on your writing?

AL A lot, because journalism teaches you economy, discipline, humor, and humility. You learn that there is no one Mount Everest. There are many Mount Everests. Secondly, you learn that you cannot wait for inspiration. You have to finish when your editor-in-chief tells you to finish. Third, it teaches you how to express yourself with respect to your readers, to use the simplest and most accurate words. But then comes a moment when you don't like it because it's repetitious, it's sort of superficial, and it doesn't let you go deep enough. But as a schooling, I would recommend it. It helped.

And then, you know, when you have books, people like

actors and actresses say, "Why don't you write a play?" and
musicians say, "Why don't you write a cantata or a symphony?" So I did. I asked, "How should I do it?" One man
showed me. "Look, I will tell you how Janacek did it with
Dostoyevsky. He took *Notes from Underground*, in a Jewish
way, from back to the beginning, and found some fine sentences, some nice paragraphs, and based his music on it. So
you tell me, what are the most important images in your
book *Night and Hope* and I will compose a symphony." He
was a student of Janacek. I did it and he wrote a composition.
We—he—won all the prizes, first in the Prague Music
Spring. It was produced on records. Then one man came and
said to me, in America, "We have this exhibition, 'Precious
Legacy.' Can you write a cantata for it?" I asked what kind of
cantata. He said a cantata which would respect the Jewish
things which are now only content for a museum because the
people who owned them are dead. I said I would try. I did it in
an afternoon. Pepe, my son, translated it in seven hours and
we had a cantata called *Shames from Prague*, which was
performed by symphonic orchestras in New Orleans, Cleveland, here in Washington, D.C., and still has some life, maybe. But it's only through the books.

First and most important is to write stories and to have, at
least once every two years, a book published. I am happy to
work and I can try whatever: a puppet show, if you should
ask. Because to write is to play, too. It's not only this terrible
responsibility. It is also play, it's very pleasant. It keeps me
younger, at least inside. And you have to do it because you
have a brain that doesn't permit you to do anything else. You
would be a bum if you don't write. I don't know who I would
be if I wouldn't write. It gives me some value in my own eyes
and this is what we need: beauty, meaning, stability—three
most important qualities of life as mentioned by Franz Joseph
Kafka. Purpose of being. Perhaps it's an illusion.

HJC Czechoslovakia seems right now to have a number
of fine artists. You mentioned Janacek and there are Passer,
Forman, and others like Hrabal, Havel, Vaculik, Kundera,

Skvorecky, and people like that. Is that number of writers disproportionate?

AL   No, no. I think it's a good country, a very inspiring land. You have only to walk in the Jewish quarter of Prague. It's stimulating. I feel like walking there every day. I don't have to be there to feel that way. It's an inspiring atmosphere for writers even from a distance. And even when you know you will never go back, maybe. Kafka, Hasek, Capek—but you cannot live only with writers. You need bakers and shoemakers. You need everything, and the older I am the more I respect the many people who are doing such things.

HJC   Tell me, what has America meant to you?

AL   In the beginning, it was a strange country, where I planned to spend at most a year, just like I did in Yugoslavia and in Israel. I was in New York writing a screenplay about Janusz Korczak for Jan Kadar, who was the director of *Shop on Main Street*. (It had been my idea to make this story into a film.) Now I have a story about Korczak in a book, *Street of Lost Brothers*. It's not only inspiration—it's a deep love. Kadar originally brought me there for six weeks. In Yugoslavia, I was writing a screenplay about Marshal Tito. After a year working here, I discovered that America is not such a bad place at all. I really came with a fear about what America is— brutality in the air. And the longer I stay here, the more I like it; it is a most free country. In England there is also freedom, but there you cannot meet a lord as simply. It would be an exception. Here, while you don't meet Rockefeller every day, you may. If you buy a refrigerator, it is probably the same kind the U.S. president has. There is really freedom for all, and Americans are obsessed with freedom. But they are also somehow obsessed with slavery and with fear of defeat. Anybody can make you a slave if you allow it—but the moment you object, nobody pushes you anymore.

They give you a minimum wage and tell you, "You know, when my grandfather came he worked harder than you," and so on; everybody wants to see you work like his grandfather. And everybody is scared of defeat. Therefore so much talk about victory. But it's only an upside-down turned horror of defeat. So there are these two sides to America. But I have never before seen a country which is so free, where working people can make a living so comfortably. I appreciate if you don't feel cold, if you eat three times a day, if you have a roof over your head, if you don't fear when there is a knock on your door that it is the Gestapo or the KGB or the Czech police. It's really a beautiful country. But, you know, you cannot praise any country too much. Firstly, it can change, and secondly, somebody can hit you on the street. Somewhere there are criminals in the government, somewhere on the streets. It's a beautiful country, very free. But also free for criminals. There is a concept of justice which I really like in America. Americans prefer not killing a criminal in case he is an innocent man. This I like very much. It's also a very legalistic country, which I don't like so much because most of my life I saw laws without justice, as I said. But here it's possible that when laws are unjust, you can fight them.

So I like America, as you see. And I am happy that I can say it from all my heart. It's not propaganda. It's not lies. It's not politeness. It's better than I expected. I had planned on leaving after a year and I've been here eighteen years. And I will stay. And to have American papers? They were the very first real papers in my life. My American passport made me a part of a great community which is ready to defend itself. When I came back from my first trip abroad and a black girl smiled at me at the airport, I really felt at home—more—I felt safe. It has dignity of a simple life, safe for all. So is a writing without that kind of fear which I hate.

HJC   Tell me something about your writing routine.

AL   I write every second I can. If I have to, I get up at 4:00 and I write for as long as my brain goes on working. When it stops working, so do I, because you have to slow down. But I really fill all my time with writing. Writing is the greatest pleasure for me. It's alcohol, love-making, good food—plus it has better results.

HJC   So you don't write set amounts a day, or even at specific times of day?

AL No. I write every second I can. And you know, if you are an older writer, you are like an old horse in a mine. Even if I am not writing, I'm writing. Even as I speak to you, I am thinking about what will happen two hours later when I sit down to write.

HJC I talked to one of your students, who confirmed what I saw in your writings, namely, that you don't concentrate on the totally painful side of the camp experience.

AL It's not necessary. Look at Sophocles and all those old Greeks. There were horrible things they were describing, like a man killing—not knowingly—his father and sleeping with his mother, and finding out, blinding himself. Never atrocities—this is for history. Not for poetry. You have to get tragedy into some chamber of the human mind where it will stay forever. And atrocity can stay there, but it can't inspire. It only scares. So this is the humanity of writing, of creative writing. You can find it in Sophocles or the others.

HJC In a talk I gave I noted that, like Greek tragedy, all of the atrocities in your stories take place off stage.

AL This is exactly what happens. I don't like the atrocities. I feel sick describing them, as I felt sick looking at them. I do describe it, but then I cut it out. I know it doesn't belong there. If they were to publish the first version of a story I am now writing, it would be there. But I will cut it out. It's about a boy, twenty years old, after the war. He serves in the military and his commander doesn't like Jews. He sends him for a special mission and he falls with an avalanche into an abyss. And during one second, everything he has experienced in his life, not only in camp, but including the camp, comes together. Because life is really a river, as old Talmudists believe. There is no beginning and no end, no time—[no] beginning—[no] middle and [no] end—a flow from nowhere to nowhere. Only we are trying to put some order in. Originally, I put in all the atrocities he experienced in life. But then I cut them out. The story will not contain atrocities.

HJC Yes, but you have the story of the young boy who has to knock his dead father's golden teeth out in *Diamonds of the Night.*

AL But this is beautiful. The boy did the best he could under the circumstances. I will tell you how I wrote it. One year after the war, we were working in Radio Prague as young reporters. We had a picnic with girls and beer and barbecue (Czech style). Everybody was happy except him. His name was H.A. We went to school together. I knew him well. He lost all his family. And he said, "You know, there is no one to tell." And he told me the story. He said they were in Lodz, Litzmanstadt. Hunger, beating, cold, fear, horrible circumstances. His father had just died. He had to do it because his mother was dying, his sister was dying. He was scared they would take the corpse away and steal the gold teeth. (He spoiled my evening, too.) I told him, "Look, I am happy it didn't happen to me. But I swear to God that you did the only right thing and if I had been in your situation, I would have done the same." The next day, I brought him the story. I couldn't sleep, you know, so I wrote it. And he said that it was exactly how it had happened. It was published and awarded in Bohemia, in Prague, in Australia, as the best story of the year. You can now get the book from Jonathan Brent of Northwestern University Press. They improved the translation a little. So I am very happy with that story.

HJC When did you decide you were going to be a writer?

AL Immediately after the war. There was too much in me, a danger of explosion. You know, only after the war things started moving together. And the whole picture looked worse and worse. Only I didn't have an education. I gave myself ten, fifteen years to catch up. So I became a journalist and enlisted in the university. I wrote my first novel. And you know what happened? They accepted it.

HJC Which book was that?

AL A novel, 350 pages. The last words were: "Nevermore war." But when the publisher in Prague accepted it, I was not so sure. I had a discussion with my friend. He said, "Look, the problem is the writer doesn't have to be the most clever in the world. But he should be the most responsible. What if you are the last? Did you say it all?" I was nineteen years old. So I went to the publishing house and I said, "Give it back to me."

They said, "Why?" I said, "Because I feel that I can do better."
They said, "But it's good and ready to go to print and we never
had a case that a young writer. . . . It is good." I said, "Look,
it's about dead people, so I have to feel comfortable." I made
seven stories out of it: *Night and Hope*. In the meantime,
Stalin was in power and he didn't like Jews and didn't like
suffering. You know, under Stalin, everything in arts and
propaganda became like a Hollywood movie. Everybody had
to sing and nobody could be sad—happy endings to everything. But the people with the publishing house knew about
it, and the moment a more liberal era began, they published it
immediately. It was a happy book, I must tell you. It was
published several times, and made into a film, *Transport from
Paradise*. Now it's out again through Northwestern University Press in it's fifth edition. It was first published by Dutton
in New York in America in 1962.

HJC In *Darkness Casts No Shadow*, at the very end, are
the boys shot or do they live?

AL According to all the rules of Aristotle, they must die
because it's a tragedy. It would be otherwise no tragedy. I am
one of them, I did not have the heart to shoot myself, maybe I
am superstitious. I was in the situation of the mock execution. They let us go into the woods believing that we would
starve and die like wolves. I wanted to indicate that they did
die, but I couldn't say it because I felt that it was like committing suicide. There is a difference between life and a story.
The story has its own rules. And in the story the boys have to
die. Historically, it's the truth. It has nothing to do with my
private truth. The rule of tragedy is death.

HJC Do you work on one book at a time?

AL I write like it's a workshop. Now I feel good because I
would take it hard if my novels hadn't been published. I
wanted *Diamonds* most of all, then *Prayer for Katerina Horo-
vitoza* and the others. They all got nice reviews—in the *New
York Times*, and the *Chicago Tribune, Washington Post, San
Francisco Chronicle*. Never a bad one. But nothing much
happened. Or—who knows how it works? Fame always dis-
appears. Like if you throw a stone into a lake. It makes a few

circles, then there is deep silence again. What remains is meaning. The memory also loses colors, details, and so on, and what remains from and in memory is the meaning. Literature is the emotional memory of man. So the meaning is important. No? So are you going to make my books better known? It would be nice. But didn't I say we have to be patient? And then, writers are really never satisfied. But maybe some of the readers are. And life is always a circle. So, 'till the next book. 'Till the next reader.

SIMON WIESENTHAL

Simon Wiesenthal was a prisoner in a Nazi concentration camp for over four years. He has helped to establish important survivor organizations. Before founding the world-famed Jewish Documentation Center in Vienna, he established a similar institution in Linz, Austria, which flourished from 1947 to 1954. Their objective was to bring war criminals to justice. He also established the Wiesenthal Center for Holocaust Studies in Los Angeles.

Born in Galicia, he attended the Universities of Prague and Lemberg in Poland, where he was an architect before the war broke out. When he regained his freedom he was employed by the War Crimes Commission, the U.S. Office of Strategic Service, and the Counter-Intelligence Corps (1945-1947). From 1954 to 1961 Wiesenthal directed several Jewish welfare agencies in Linz. He has served as president of the Association of Jews Persecuted by the Nazis and as vice-president of both the Union International des Resistent et Deportés (Brussels) and the Federal Association of Jewish Communities of Austria. His books published in English include *The Murderers among Us* (1967), *The Sunflower* (1976), the novel *Max and Helen* (1982), and *Every Day Remembrance Day* (1986). Wiesenthal has received much world-wide recognition, including the Congressional Gold Medal, the Diploma of Honour from the League of Nations, the Jerusalem Medal, the Freedom Medals of the Netherlands and Luxembourg. He was also named Commandeur of Orange-Nassau and Commentatore de la Republica Italiana. Wiesenthal has been awarded a number of honorary degrees from such institutions as Hebrew Union College, Colby College, John Jay College of Criminal Justice of the City University of New York, and Hebrew Theological College.

HJC   Why are you engaged in tracking down Nazi criminals?

SW   There is a great danger that young people—and I mean young men and women in general, not just those who are Jewish—think that our disaster began with Hitler. I feel that we should look at the Holocaust as the end of perhaps a two thousand-year process. In my work I am not only trying to find Nazis and bring them to justice; I am also looking for answers for myself. I went back through the centuries, every century of our existence, to try to find out what was done to us. From this examination I have established six components of our tragedy. I believe that this holds true not only for the Jewish tragedy but for the massacres of other innocent people, like the Armenians, the Gypsies, and religious and racial minorities.

HJC   The components each became a chapter heading in the book you have just completed, I believe.

SW   Yes. First is hatred. That is obvious and does not need elaboration. Dictatorship is second. Over the centuries this has been a variable—it could be a king, an emperor, a pope, archbishop or bishop, a general, a president. In other words, people of power. Component number three is bureaucracy. By this I mean not only people sitting behind desks. For me it's men in execution squads, those who operate gas chambers, the murderers. I call them bureaucrats because they follow orders. Without them dictatorship and hatred could not have strong "value." Next is technology. Hatred needs technology for the annihilation of people. I believe that if those who implemented the Spanish Inquisition had had the technology that was available to Hitler, the Jews would not have been offered the alternative to be baptized or die, [or] to be baptized or emigrate in some cases. In the religious persecutions, no Jew would have survived in Spain, no Protestant would have escaped France, perhaps no Catholic would have remained alive in England. Component number five is a period of crisis. Looking through history we find that genocides—massacres—happen in times of war, of crisis. The Turks could slaughter the Armenians only during war. In war a country is closed, everything is kept secret. Believe me, Hitler had studied the holocaust of the Armenians very carefully. In a time of crisis there is a need for scapegoats. A diversion has to be made from those who are actually guilty for the unhappy situation. Throughout the centuries Jews have been the number one scapegoats of nations in trouble. The final component, the sixth, is the need for a minority—whether it be a social, ethnic, religious, political, or racial group.

HJC You have completed another book recently, have you not?

SW I have. It is a story about the Polish resistance and has very little to do with Jews. But as you know—we have spoken about this before—my dream is of a brotherhood of victims. Many Jews do not understand this. I wrote a story of the Polish resistance primarily because after the war the Communists have falsified the story of Polish resistance to the Nazis. The national Polish resistance was 95 percent of the resistance and began one month after the occupation of Poland by the German forces. The Communist resistance started two years after the Nazis had won over Soviet territory. I have discovered very important documents. One month after the Ribbentrop-Molotov Pact it was published with the signatures of the two officials. They met again and made an additional treaty for a common fight against Polish resistance.

HJC This will have important implications for Polish Communists.

SW Of course. I found letters from Katyn dated April 14,

1940, and November 14, 1940, letters sent by the International Red Cross to camps in Russia where Polish officers were imprisoned. The letters were returned with cancellations from the Soviet post office at the camp indicating that the individuals were no longer in the camp. When you compare that information with the list of Polish officers found by the Nazis to have been murdered in Katyn, you have them.

HJC   This is new information.

SW   Yet it is. I published a portion of it in *Der Spiegel*. It didn't make a very deep impression. These are documents which the Soviets cannot deny. Let me tell you about how I learned some of the things I know. In 1945, when I was liberated, I weighed about ninety pounds. I recovered slowly and I heard witnesses every day telling their terrible stories. So I prolonged my time in the concentration camp so I could leave with not only my own story but the stories of what happened to many others. They shared their experiences and I so identified with their stories that I wept with them. Sometimes when I am a witnes in a case, I tell the judge frankly that while I was in the same camp as the accused, I may not have personally seen some of the things other witnesses tell about, but I can remember what people told me at the time of liberation. All of the judges say that they have never heard a witness diminish my testimony. I may have actually observed some of the atrocities but I cannot be one hundred percent certain of the details, and I admit that. For me, the personal truth, the historical truth, is of absolute importance.

HJC   Just let me tell you a quick story. Jean Piaget, the Swiss psychologist, told in his autobiography the story about how he used to describe his having been kidnapped as a child. He was very young. It happened when his household companion, the maid, took him for a walk one afternoon. He described the kidnapper, he described the events. Years later he found out that it never occurred. She had made up this story to cover meeting her lover and she told it so often and so well that he thought he had actually experienced it. So clearly the mind plays tricks, and of course you are right in warning that you cannot be certain if you actually saw or heard about certain events.

SW   I was educated in the home. My grandparents were very, very religious. Two days ago in Cleveland I spoke with rabbis concerning this demagoguery which I cannot understand around the person of Waldheim. We all knew that he's not a friend of Jews, he's not a friend of Israel. The one who attacks Waldheim with such hatred is killing the case. Nobody will believe him, they see he is a hater. The documents will be very hard, the language should be moderate—let the people make the conclusion. It is my whole way since '45. I remember I was a small child when I heard a discussion. Somebody was talking about Jewish ethics regarding what I think of as a great sin. Innocent men who were Jews were connected with a capital crime. This was a terrible accusation, but that this accusation was true was at the same time a terrible sin. You know how holy human life is for Jews. We say, "Who saves one life saves the whole world." To accuse somebody—without evidence—I would never do. And I've been involved in three thousand cases. That Waldheim is innocent, I cannot guarantee. But I have no evidence that he committed crimes. I know that he is not telling the truth in a few cases, small things. But I never call him a liar, because when you call someone a liar it means that he lied his whole life. When someone sues me, I'll bring a hundred examples that he is lying and he's still not a liar. During my lectures people ask me about Waldheim and I say, "Yes, the man in a number of cases is not telling the truth, but there is no evidence that he committed crimes, though they put him on a list of war criminals." Accusation is not a proof. But here some people wish to play both prosecutor and judge.

HJC   When I met you the first time, here in St. Louis at a private luncheon to which I was invited, I didn't want to go. I said to myself, this is a man who must be consumed by hatred. I obviously didn't know.

SW   Never, never. Only in the first few months after the war. But for me that whole world is guilty—in an absolutely other sense—not only those who killed our families but also those people who looked away, who accepted that we have no right to live. Those people looked on us as subhuman. But, in thinking, I concluded that guilt is individual, guilt is not collective. Historical events in Germany, in France, in Spain, show that the Jews were, for thousands of years the victims of collective guilt. They made the Jews responsible for what one Jew had done or what ten Jews had done. In this place or the other place the Jews were always seen as guilty. I come from a religious home, [but] I am not a practicing Jew who goes every day to a synagogue and so on. My religion is the ethics part of the religion. (This ethics is also part of other religions that came later. Without our ethics they have not their ethics.) In the 50s I had my first interview on TV in Germany. The man who interviewed me was a former priest. The first question was, "Are you for collective guilt or not?" I said absolutely not.

HJC   What influence did your experience in writing *The Sunflower* have on your attitude about collective guilt?

SW   Absolutely no influence. I learned from my previous experience that not all ten and a half million Nazi party members were criminals. Probably less than 2 percent were involved in actual crimes. I invited the Nazi head of a railway repair shop to the wedding of my daughter in Holland. I worked for him when I was a prisoner and I watched how he operated. When he learned that some of his German employees from the railway were beating Jews, he sent those Germans to the front. He spoke with me a few times.

Furthermore, my two-year experience in the Soviet Union taught me how people can finish their studies or keep to their work and not go into the party. I recognized two types: party members and Nazis. There was a large difference. After the war, one of the best prosecuting attorneys in Germany said to me: "Before somebody else tells you, I will tell you. I was a Nazi myself. I had to finish two more years of study and I was told that unless I became a Nazi I would not be allowed to complete my studies. What could I do? I was from a very poor family, so I joined the party." He said that "even with membership in the party I was no Nazi. I was never a Nazi." I understood that in a dictatorship the atmosphere of terror could bring people to party membership.

HJC Did any of the people that you asked to contribute to *The Sunflower* refuse with hostile letters or anything like that?

SW No, no. But some people, like Hochhuth (and I wrote him twice) never even sent an answer.

HJC I had the same experience with him on a project I was working on.

SW I should tell you that there are more contributors in other language editions than in the English edition. It was published in sixteen languages and with world-famous people, and we also added a number of local people. In the Italian edition we have some Communists. The German edition includes Albert Speer.

HJC Really?

SW Sure. This is very, very important. The American publisher of *The Sunflower* wouldn't print him. You understand this prejudice?

HJC Yes. That's fascinating. It would be important to know what Speer thought about your silence in the matter.

SW He absolutely agreed with me. Coming back to Hochhuth. He told me that he had written three different responses. He was not very happy with any of them. Then I talked to him and said, "Look, don't make another." Because what everybody wrote is a credo—they can never in their whole life change it. I talked with S.Y. Agnon. He is from my home town. He was the best friend of my late uncle. I told him the story and I asked him if he wished to say something. He said he believed that I handled the problem with good instinct. Another man who also refused was Klaus Gruber. He said, "Look, this was like a confession and I am not going to comment on any confessions."

Believe me, until now after so many years, I will say only this: I'm not a hundred percent sure that I handled the event the right way. Maybe only ninety-nine percent sure—because of the argument of a comrade who was with me in the same bed in Mathausen. He said to me, "You see this was not a typical adventure." But he had time to think about it. What could we do? I should say nothing. I am not authorized. I am authorized to forgive when he does something against me. Here you have a glimpse of the ethics of the two religions. A Jewish rabbi will never say *ego te absolvo*. And this absolution developed through the generations to be something of a routine. I never heard of a priest with a dying murderer without this man saying he is sorry for what he has done. But in any case there are some people who say that a person feels better when he can talk to you. Even when you are silent you understand him. You do not forgive him with words. The fact is that later I went to his mother and I did not tell her the whole story. He was for me a victim of the times. So I very, very often come back to *The Sunflower*, because this is an eternal problem. In five hundred years it will be the same, and five hundred years ago it was the same. It is a problem of human relations. I have written a number of books; not all of them are in English. I feel that this is my best book. Because I put [forth] a question—the question is more important than the answer.

HJC   Did you say your best book?

SW   Absolutely the best book. This is a small segment of my life—but an important segment, a very, very important segment.

HJC   Speaking about the segment of your life: *The Murderers among Us*, was that your idea in the book or was it Wexberg's idea?

SW   This book I wrote in German. My literary agent said we are appealing to a big American audience.

HJC   This section originated in English.

SW   Yes. So I brought all this that I had written in German to Wexberg. He was a man who was very, very sensitive and sometimes when I was telling the story, both of us cried. He edited my stories, he made them readable. He did not contribute one idea to this, he merely edited.

HJC   And finally, let me ask you about *Max and Helen*. Where did that come from? Is that a true story?

SW   One hundred percent so. I must tell you. Max could

still be alive, but he committed suicide. I would never have
written that book if he were living—I absolutely would not. I
had long talks with Helen. We changed some names so that
her son should not recognize himself. You know what happened? After this book was published in Scandinavia an
engineer came from Sweden, a Jew, and said, "Mr. Wiesenthal, you wrote my story. The commander was my father. My
mother died two years ago of cancer and before her death she
told me the story. The commander was my father and under
her influence he changed—so that in '44 when he got the
order to kill all the Jews, he took me and some others out and
told us to disappear." There was also a bigger camp than this
camp, and four hundred Jews were saved. I had him arrested
for other crimes, not for those activities. This is the man in
the book of *The Murderers among Us*—Rokita. He never
killed somebody face to face. He would drop a piece of paper
and say, "Please pick it up." When the man bent over, he shot
him. I found him in Hamburg. But he never went to trial. He
was so sick that he died in prison from illness.

HJC Rokita?

SW Yes. And this year I found another witness from the
same camp in Haifa. He wrote me a letter saying that he had
worked on that road and he gave me additional information
beyond what Helen and Max gave me For instance, that in
many cases they brought stones—gravestones from the Jewish cemetery—to destroy them for the building of the road.

Max and Helen is now being made into a film, so I gave this
new information to those people making the film because I
now have a witness for it. You understand, this is not an
invention.

YITZHAK ARAD

Dr. Yitzhak Arad was one of the legendary resistance fighters of the Jewish Underground during World War II. Though barely beyond the age of childhood, he escaped from the Jewish ghetto at Vilna, Lithuania, and became an active combatant and a leader of this movement, fighting in the forests of Belorussia until the war's end. His parents and family perished in the Holocaust.

After the Nazi surrender, Arad fled to and illegally entered Eretz Israel. He volunteered for combat in the underground Palmah and later served in the Israel Defense Forces where he had various command responsibilities until 1972. His highest rank was that of brigadier general. Upon discharge from the military, Arad was appointed chairman of the Yad Vashem Holocaust Remembrance Authority in Jerusalem. He earned a doctorate in history from the University at Tel Aviv, where he became a lecturer in Jewish history. His book *Ghetto in Flames* (1976), based on his doctoral dissertation, is a chronicle of the Jews in Vilna between 1941 and 1945. A subsequent volume, *Belzec, Sobibor, Treblinka,* (1987) tells of the murders of over a million Jews at the three infamous concentration camps located in Poland under the code-name Operation Reinhard. He has also published many articles on the history of the Holocaust.

HJC Your reputation as one of the great resistance fighters is widespread. Would you say something about your experience in and around Vilna at that time?

YA Initially I was in the ghetto underground movement from 1942 until 1944. Then I joined the partisans until the end of the war. We fought against the Germans and their collaborators.

HJC How old were you then?

YA When the war started I was not yet thirteen. I began my underground activity at fifteen.

HJC How did you become involved in that?

YA The Germans occupied my native town of Swieciany, which had about 3,000 Jews, at the end of July '41. In September they told all of the Jews that they were being removed to a ghetto. A total of about 8,000 Jews were taken—not to a ghetto but to an isolated military camp instead. They shot them on the second day. I escaped.

HJC How did you get away?

YA The night before we were deported from Swieciany to the so-called ghetto a group of us fifteen- to sixteen-year-olds decided to flee to Belorussia. Life for Jews there was (relative to those of us in Lithuania) much different. There were no mass killings, no ghettos. We did not know that we were escaping annihilation but we learned a few days after our arrival in Belorussia that Eisatzgruppen Eight murdered our people. Only 250 remained. They were skilled workers—tailors, shoemakers, carpenters—who were forced to work for the Germans. But after a few months the killing of Jews began in Belorussia. So I left there and returned to my native town. There I was captured by the Germans and taken out of the ghetto with about ten others. We thought they would shoot us because we didn't have any documents. However, they took us to a place outside of town where there was a camp where they collected captured Soviet arms. We were put to cleaning the weapons. On the first day I put a small gun beneath my shirt without knowing if I'd be searched at the end of the day. I wasn't and was able to bring it back to Swieciany that night. We continued to work this way for about a month, and I and my friends were able to steal about ten guns. So we started an underground group. In February 1943 we left for the forest, and our group operated for about two months.

HJC How many were you?

YA There were twenty-five youngsters. It was very, very hard to do very much. In the forest the local population was not collaborating with Jews. In order to survive in the forest you must have support from the local people—to get information about the enemy, to get some help with food. But they would immediately inform the Germans where we were, and peasants can always find you in the forest. It was very difficult; but in about two months we met up with a Russian partisan group and we joined with them.

HJC They were non-Jews?

YA Yes, non-Jews. It was the Markov Brigade. They had just come from the East, in a westward direction. Within another two months a Lithuanian Communist parachute group was sent to our area. These were Lithuanian Communists who escaped from the Soviet Union during the Russian retreat, and they were sent back to organize a partisan movement in their home country. So, as a Lithuanian citizen, I joined their ranks until 1944. I took part in blowing up sixteen German echelons. The details of these are in my book *The Partisan.*

HJC How was the relationship between you and the non-Jews in the Resistance?

YA There were many problems for a Jew to be with the Soviet partisans. First of all, there were anti-Semitic feelings. Then, a Jew would only be accepted in the ranks of the Soviet partisans if he had his own arms. (Any non-Jew, whether a local peasant or one who had escaped from a prisoner-of-war camp, would be accepted without arms.) Also, there was the image of the Jew as a bad fighter or a coward. So you fought to prove yourself, to say, "Anything you can do I can do—if not better at least as well." So in the beginning we had to struggle for our places. But after a few months I was able to prove myself—my courage—and was allowed to take part in mining many trains, in ambushes and other activities. But still it wasn't easy. There was some talk about making specifically Jewish units, but we could not do it because the official attitude of the Soviet partisan movement was that there was no place for Jewish units.

The Soviet partisan movement was organized according to the structure of the Soviet Republic: Lithuanian, Belorussian, Ukranian groups, etc. Since there was no Jewish republic, they forced us to disband. This became a problem because not all Jews were able to join partisan units. Some Jews even had their arms taken from them and had to face the danger of forest life without weapons. But as time passed and the Soviet partisan movement became better organized and more disciplined the situation of the Jews became better. In the beginning of 1943 the control over all these groups became stronger, discipline was harder, so things became improved for Jews in some way.

HJC   I take it that you mean for Jewish fighters and not for Jews in general?

YA   Yes, for the fighters. There was another problem in the forests and that was for Jewish families. Some Jews were able to escape into the forest and establish family camps. It was extremely difficult for them to survive. Such a camp usually contained a small nucleus of armed men who had to guard the others and obtain food for them. When I say get food, what does it mean? They had to go into the village and take the food by force, like the partisans did. As time passed, the food problem got worse because the peasants in the area became poorer and poorer. The partisans took from them, the Germans took from them, and those taking for the family camps had to feed the women and children as well as themselves. At the same time the Germans were increasing their activities in the forest. They brought large forces to encircle the forest. We as partisans usually knew the German moves beforehand (our reconnaissance units informed us), so we were able to break through or else disperse into small groups of two or three, infiltrate the area, and in a few weeks reunite in some distant place. The Germans would be unable to keep their troops in the forest permanently, so when they left, we returned. But mobility for families was quite limited, so of course they were the first victims. The partisan units did not want to take the families with them because it was rough to move. It was very hard on the families.

HJC   Before you young boys of fifteen and sixteen joined up with partisans, how were you able to maintain any discipline?

YA   There were two or three among us who became leaders. This was a kind of personal leadership but some had more experience, too. A couple of them were in their early twenties and one had served in the Polish army, so he knew a little more about military ways. And those who joined the group in its beginning had some status. Even as a young boy I had some authority because I was the one who brought the first arms into the ghetto.

HJC   The younger ones were willing to follow the lead of others? They recognized the need for that?

YA   Yes.

HJC   Did you know what was going on beyond your area, in the Vilna Ghetto for example?

YA   Even before we were partisans, when we were in the Swieciany underground, we had contact with the Vilna Ghetto. Later, as partisans, they asked us to leave the forest and join them in the ghetto because they planned an uprising. In April '43, I and another boy reached the Vilna Ghetto—it's a long story which I tell in my book—and we met with the leadership of their underground group, including Abba Kovner. They asked us to participate in the uprising in the ghetto. We told them that we thought they had no chance of success, that such an act would be just another way to die. We told them to organize as many youths as possible, instead, and leave the ghetto to unite with us in the forest. This was my final personal contact with the ghetto. Some of our other boys continued to be in contact with them and eventually some did leave the Vilna Ghetto to come with us. After the uprising—which occurred in September 1943—others from the Jewish underground there came with us, too. Part of them reached the area where I operated, in the Narocz forest. Some of them went south of Vilna, to the Rudnicki forest.

HJC How does one who had participated so long and so courageously in the battle against the Nazis react to the charges that the Jews did not resist, did not fight back?

YA Look, such charges are based on a misunderstanding of the situation of the Jews at that time and of not knowing of the existing Jewish Resistance. The main problem of the Jewish Resistance then, I would say, was that the way to the forest was open only for young men who could get arms and fight in the forest. For the Jewish masses—women, children, elderly people—there was no way. I was without a family, without children, so it wasn't a question for me. But I ask myself today, "If I had been twenty-four or twenty-five, married, and with two children in the ghetto, what would I have done?" I might have been working, say, in some German factory. That gave us a little security, a way to get food for my family. And I would live like others in the ghetto, hoping that some miracle might happen. Maybe Hitler would be killed, maybe the Allied forces would land in a second-front assault, maybe Germany would collapse, or there would be a successful Russian offensive. People lived with some hopes. Maybe as a young man I might have possibly escaped to the forest with some guns and left my wife and children behind in order to fight and blow up some German trains or something.

I have asked myself many times, "What would have been the right thing to do? What does courage mean in this situation?" If you go out to fight and destroy things, you leave your family helpless. At the first selection or first *aktion* they become immediate victims. Even before that they will suffer from lack of food. If you stay with them you hope you will survive together. Which is the most courageous choice? When I lecture in Israel, I raise this question—asking army men, cadets, officers, "What would have been the right thing to do?" Silence. How can one answer? I behaved one way as a young man and I do not have to justify my activity, so I can ask the question. If people escaped from the ghetto they went to a village, to a second village, to the forest to try to survive. But they were most usually caught either by local collaborators or someone informing the Germans or the Lithuanian police. Very few had a chance to reach the forest. Fighting gave very little chance for surviving. And the main aim of the Jews at that time, I would say, was to survive. The Jewish victory would be in survival. Some might try to prolong their existence by hiding, others by escaping to the forest. Some chose to remain in the ghetto, to try to make it more productive with the hope that there would be a chance to survive that way. All the ways were right ways. Today when we look at the Judenrat, we think it did not prove itself in working life. But if we look at it from the point of view of 1942 or '43, what else could they have done? It was the only way.

HJC   In your book *Ghetto in Flames* you say that the Judenrat you knew about did the best they could.

YA   Yes, the best they could. No other real policy was open for the Jews at that time.

HJC   Let me ask you a different kind of question: What has it meant to you to be the director of Yad Vashem?

YA   I came to Israel illegally, in a small boat on Christmas night in 1945. I was active in the underground, against the British. In some way, I pushed the Holocaust out of my consciousness. But when I came back to the Event, I came with all of my energy—not for eight hours of work a day but twenty-four. I came to Yad Vashem as a historian, as a teacher. I have this obligation to the people who were less lucky than myself. In order to survive, in addition to everything you did, you needed some luck. If you are religious you can say you needed God's help. What I am doing at Yad Vashem is my obligation to those who did not survive. Fate enabled me to live, and I must do something to commemorate the war, to write about it, to make it more understandable to people. I think there are many lessons from the Holocaust, for us as Jews, for human beings in general—there is a whole universal meaning. If, in some way, I succeed in doing something in this direction—to promote more awareness, more knowledge, the lessons that should be learned—this is for me a great satisfaction.

HJC I have seen you work, I am involved with it in a small way, and you are succeeding very well.

YA Thank you very much.

MORDECAI PALDIEL

In 1982, Dr. Mordecai Paldiel was appointed Director of the Department for the Righteous at Yad Vashem, the Holocaust memorial authority in Jerusalem. His duty as director is to oversee the investigations of cases in which non-Jews are nominated to be recognized for heroism in aiding Jews during the Shoah.

Paldiel was born in Antwerp to a family of Polish origin. They fled to the Italian-occupied zone in France, and in 1943, with the assistance of a French priest, they escaped to neutral Switzerland. He emigrated to the United States in 1956 and then to Israel six years later. He earned a B.A. in political science at Hebrew University, then an M.A. and Ph.D. in religion from Temple University in Philadelphia. His dissertation was entitled "Dualism and Genocide: The 'Religious' Nature of Hitler's Antisemitism." Dr. Paldiel taught Hebrew and Judaic studies at a Philadelphia high school as a graduate student and served as director of the Israel Histadrut Foundation (Philadelphia and Miami) from 1974 to 1977. His articles have appeared in *Midstream, The Journal of Ecumenical Studies, Holocaust and Genocide Studies, The Jerusalem Post,* and *Yakut Moreshet.* He was a visiting professor at Stockton State College in New Jersey in 1991. His book, *The Path of the Righters* (1992), is about Christian rescuers.

HJC What has your work meant to you personally?

MP My work at Yad Vashem these past six years has opened for me a new understanding of human nature; one of which I had no inkling, no knowledge. I never imagined that there was such a dimension to human behavior. I would put it in a few words: it's the possibility, the capability of caring for the other person with no tangible ulterior motive, for nothing that would benefit the agent or the doer of good deeds. I did not imagine that such type of behavior is possible other than for the very select group of saints, "lamed vovniks," or persons who are not within the normal stream of social life. I have discovered that there are thousands of people who live in various countries of Europe, who come from different walks of life, and carry with them a bag of prejudices and stereotyped feelings about other ethnic groups, yet are capable of overcoming these feelings in order to do singular, unique acts of goodness—namely, the saving of human lives at the risk of their own, helping others to survive, and then going on with their daily lives. This discovery has been, personally, very uplifting—to know that there is a dimension of goodness which, perhaps, is intrinsic in human behavior. The agents of these good deeds themselves are completely unaware that there is anything untoward or anything exceptional about what they did—that is another good sign. They explain their behavior as normal—anything but abnormal. They don't consider themselves heroes for having risked their lives to save human beings under the most unimaginable conditions possible. If these people could have done that [then] I can identify with them. I can see in them the reflection of myself as a person with strengths and weaknesses, with good sides, perhaps not so pleasant sides. I can identify with them and it leaves a measure of hope for the future of humanity.

HJC Is there a common thread that motivated these people, or is that too simple to suggest?

MP Perhaps it would be simplistic to find a common thread in the thousands of those that we have already on record but we have to make the attempt. What I have found out is that the overwhelming majority of these people were able to put aside the social restraints which dictate our daily lives and which dictate that we do not inconvenience ourselves too much. Certainly we do not play with our lives, certainly not with the lives of our loved ones, for the sake of others, perhaps a despised minority. If we do help, if we do show acts of altruism, it is only at a price of a slight inconvenience. That is socially acceptable. I find that these persons, no matter what their backgrounds are, were able to put such considerations in the freezer, perhaps did not think out rationally what they were actually doing because what they did was arational (I'm not using the term irrational but arational). It was not fully thought out but they were able to detach themselves from these constraints and play with the highest stakes that a person can play—one's own life and freedom in order in save other persons—persons they may have known as acquaintances informally, persons they may have met during the Holocaust and, in some cases, persons with whom they had a friendly relationship. The common thread, I find, is that they were able perhaps not to overlook but not even to look at the frightful prospects for themselves for what they were doing and assert then a humanity at a very profound level.

HJC   You are not suggesting that the motivation was always religious, or national?

MP   It is very difficult to answer that—what motivates a person at such a profound level. It is possible that there were various elements of motivation. It is possible that a person sheltered a Jew feeling that perhaps, after the war, he would be rewarded. It is possible that a childless couple decided to take in a child [because,] perhaps in the back of their minds, unawares, they may have felt that if the parents of that youngster did not survive they would be able to have a child whom they would love. It is possible that a priest who sheltered one, dozens, or hundreds of Jews, perhaps in the back of his mind may have hoped that some of them would accept Christianity, would convert. We don't know, we can't go that deeply, can't penetrate. What is important to point out is that these people did not precondition their generosity on these unknown elements which may have been there. They saved lives. They did not ask anything in return other than to be allowed to help. So the motivation, looking back, was humanitarian with the mixture of other motivations.

We all carry with us conscious and subconscious modes of behavior—we can never fully comprehend them. But for the edification of future generations, for other persons to know that it is possible—not necessarily to be a saint, not to have a halo around your head, not to be a lamed vovnik, to be as aggressive and competitive and have all the social norms of behavior with which we are programmed, yet not in spite of but commensurate with that—to be able to do acts of goodness and then go on with whatever you were doing before, [this] is a lesson we must teach. Go on, if you are a priest, go on and it's no contradiction but you may even try to—priests have been known, after the war, to go to great efforts to convert people, but during the war they made specific restraints on themselves not to take advantage of the situation. It is possible to show an extreme, a higher and more profound form of humanity in special circumstances and still go on with whatever you were doing before. It does not mean you have to be a saint, it does not mean you have to be in a different category of people. So the motivations may have been various but the ultimate motivation which conditioned, which finally dictated the decision—should I risk my own freedom and life in order to do this or not—I think the ultimate motivation must have been a humanitarian dimension of unprecedented magnanimity.

HJC And beyond risking their lives they even put in jeopardy the lives of their loved ones in many cases.

MP Of course. In eastern Europe it was very well known (bulletin boards made it clear to the population in their own language) that anyone who would as much as frustrate the Nazi design on Jews—not only giving shelter but even in transporting a Jew from one place to another, providing food—the penalty would be death, and that was spelled out in German and the local language. It was very clear. Death to

the individual and—to be honest with the record—it didn't
spell out the family but most people knew that among those
who were apprehended, in some cases, the family would be
burned in their own house, which means all of them perished. In some cases the offender and his wife might be
placed against a wall and shot and then the children would be
sent to Germany to be reeducated or to be dispersed. Their
property would be confiscated, the whole family would suffer in one way or another.

The same for western Europe. There the situation was not
as terrifying as in eastern Europe, but persons in western
Europe who were apprehended in helping Jews, they themselves would suffer, not their families—to be faithful to the
record. They would be carted off to concentration camps—or
shot as Uke Wesserow was shot. A Father Farker on the
French-Swiss border, who helped Jews escape into Switzerland, was arrested and shot. The other members of the mon-
astery, some of them received stiff sentences, the other ones
were released. But one of them was shot on the eve of the
liberation of the country. Those who were involved knew
that they might have to pay the ultimate price.

HJC   Is there some way that you could generalize about
people of one country, one area, being more willing to make
this sacrifice than others?

MP   I might point to countries like Belgium or France
where society—the social leadership, including the religious
hierarchy—encouraged people (certainly after 1942 when we
talk about France) not to be bystanders but to be personally
involved in order to prevent Jews from being deported. I
allude to Monsignor Sallier's famous pastoral letters and also
Bishop Teas' in southwestern France, and the dissemination
of these letters throughout France; the stand of the Italian
clergy; the stand of Cardinal Von Rohe in Belgium, who
alluded to the fact that persecution goes against Christian
tradition and gave the signal for persons to help. And being
that anti-Semitism was not as profound in western Europe as
it was in eastern Europe, perhaps it was an additional induce-
ment to people to make that great step, to make a great

existential leap and risk their lives for the sake of these Jews. In eastern Europe the humanitarianism of these people is even greater because there the clergy certainly did not take a stand in favor of the Jews. One might even make a case in the opposite direction—anti-Semitism was rife, was violent.

There's a history of anti-Semitism in eastern Europe which precedes the Nazi period. There were pogroms in the 1910s, 1920s, the 1930s in various countries in eastern Europe. Helping a Jew was not the most popular thing to do. People still find it hard to accept the fact, today in some countries in eastern Europe, that their next-door neighbors helped Jews. Jews were hated by large segments of the population. For a person to have found the strength to overcome these social restraints, and perhaps his own stereotyped opinions about the Jews, to be able to say, "I would even make the statement that these Jews perhaps deserve punishment for having killed Christ or for having done these things and those things, yet I, as a Christian, cannot allow human lives to be unjustly destroyed and therefore I will get involved"—that I believe is a high degree of, perhaps I shouldn't use the word courage, a high degree of humanity. That shows me, personally, not only the veracity of the statement in the Bible that man was created in the divine image, but I think if there were ever examples of the fulfillment of the parable of the good Samaritan, it is those people in Poland and in the Ukraine who could overcome perhaps their own inbred prejudices, as the record shows, and were willing to stake everything which was dearest to them to save Jews from destruction which they felt, somehow—without being able to formulate theologically or to philosphize what they felt—they just could not stand by and allow this to happen without them getting involved.

I would like to mention in this regard Zofia Kossak, a Catholic lady of renown in Poland, who was known before the war to be not disposed in a friendly way toward the Jews, to have written against the Jews. When she saw in 1940 what was happening she stated that as a Catholic, no matter what the Jews were worth, no matter if the Jews are to be blamed or

not, she could not stand aside and not get involved. She took
the first steps to create an underground network to help
Jewish children to find a place of refuge. That network later
on received a code word of *zygota* and hundreds of children
were spirited out of the Warsaw Ghetto and hidden with
families. This is the only underground operative of the Polish
underground which hid Jewish children. This was inspired
by a woman who was known for her anti-Jewish stance just
before the German invasion. She was able to overcome that.
She was able to see not the Jew but the human being. I think
that such examples of humanity are perhaps the closest to
the highest form a person can reach—to be able to overcome
the whole baggage of one's social prejudice, which we all
carry with us, in order to be able to see the thing that unites
us all and to be able to act on that.

HJC Your professional work is necessarily focused on
individuals. Do you have some general notions about communities like Le Chambon or even wider, like Denmark?

MP Yes. I personally prefer to emphasize the individual
who worked as a loner rather than the community. We cannot overlook the communities. In Le Chambon the community acted in unison because they had a leadership which
inspired, the leadership of André Trocme principally. There
were other pastors there. Protestants were a persecuted minority, had a history of persecution, and then to them it was
perhaps a theological decision or a religious decision that
they were going to help this other persecuted minority as
well. The whole community acted, and there is social support in that, of course. The same can be said in Denmark,
where the community acted, not so much from religious motives, but perhaps from other motives—political, national.
The Jews were seen an an integrated part of Denmark. The
Germans had promised that they would not meddle in
Danish affairs. The moment the Germans tried to round up
the Jews, the Danes saw that as the first sign that the Germans were going to dictate the internal affairs of Denmark,
and they were going to take a stand on that. Geography
helped them. Sweden was not far away and the whole Danish

underground acted in unison in order to spirit the small Jewish community out.

The same can be said for a town in Holland called Niederlander, in Trente, which was commemorated recently. The Dutch prime minister inaugurated a grove at Yad Vashem in honor of the hundreds of townspeople in Niederlander who sheltered Jews in their homes upon instruction of the Dutch underground. As I said, these people did not have to do that. They could have refused, as many of them stated. Not everyone was actually forced to take a Jew in their home, and they risked their lives, they risked their safety to save Jews. Returning to what I said originally, at Yad Vashem most of our cases are individual cases, those of people who worked on their own. Each had to look in the mirror. Each had no recourse, in some cases, had even no recourse to friends and relatives for help or advice.

HJC   There is a need for us to know of these people?

MP   Principally for two reasons. First of all because the stories are true. They happened. We are challenged to confront the Holocaust. It has been said that we cannot make a theological statement without looking Auschwitz in the eyes, and that is justifiably so. We are asked to be able to view a different planet, the planet of Auschwitz, which is a human planet, after all—even the perpetrators were human. I think we should be courageous enough to be able to look, to accept, to acknowledge the few single acts of goodness which also seem to come from a different realm of behavior and seem to mystify us at the beginning. Basically we ought to be able to demystify and see the humanity, the simplicity of goodness. I use the term simplicity of goodness because Hannah Arendt uses the term of "the banality of evil." There is simplicity of goodness which is there, which is part and parcel of intrinsic humanity, I believe.

So to state the facts: we at Yad Vashem have so far documented 4,000 stories of rescue but we use very rigorous criteria. Surely there are thousands and thousands more, which perhaps do not meet Yad Vashem's criteria, of people who saved Jews in various countries of Europe. The story has to be told because it happened. These are true stories. But above and beyond that, there are lessons to be drawn. We live in a human society; we have a vision of the character of the future. Everything that we know about history is about people who used the past in order to lay groundwork for some kind of future. We are all future-oriented, for good or bad. Even the Nazis with their demonic ideology were looking forward to a racially pure world.

I think there is something in the deeds of the Righteous persons which forces us to take a closer look at ourselves, at our potentials, and the stories of these Righteous can guide us in order to create a more balanced typology of human behavior. That is, not to be a Righteous person throughout one's whole life but to continue to be what we are as we are conditioned—competitive, aggressive—to leave the door open, to know of what I am capable. Don't rule yourself out just because you are such an aggressive salesman, wanting to step on another one's toes to get ahead in life—you are as capable, the possibility is there because these people were as you, many of them can fit into your role. But they somehow found a way to not allow this to interfere in their other lives and they confirmed acts for which there was no tangible reward possible. They could have ruined their lives and their freedom. The possibility is there, and if people can be made aware of that, then perhaps we can lay the groundwork for something better in human relationships and human responsiveness. I think there is something here to be learned. We ought to maximize these thousands and thousands—I'm not saying tens of thousands, certainly not hundreds of thousands—of cases. The greatest sin would be to allow these stories just to gather dust and do nothing with them. If we see so much of evil on T.V., in the movies, and in stories, and if we write so much about Mengele and Hitler and the Damjanyuks and so on, wouldn't it be a measure of justice to be fascinated by those who did acts of goodness?

HJC   You have warned that we have to do this with caution.

MP   If we applaud these people too strenuously and practically worship them, maybe we are doing not only a disservice to them (because they don't view themselves in such light), perhaps we are doing a disservice to ourselves. Perhaps what we are saying is, "These people are in a different category." We will praise them and so forth but certainly we do not see ourselves as belonging to that category of persons. We know we cannot act that way. We need these persons, they are an insignificant minority, we will hail and praise them, but we will go back to our ways. This is the wrong conclusion and people who come to that conclusion I believe have missed the whole point. The good people in their simple behavior, address themselves to us.

JAN KARSKI

For his extraordinary efforts to assist Jews during the Holocaust, Jan Karski, a Polish Catholic diplomat, was recognized as an authentic hero and benefactor by Yad Vashem, where a tree bearing his name was planted in the "Alley of the Righteous Gentiles among the Nations."

He earned two master's degrees from the University of Lvov in 1935 (in Law and Diplomatic Sciences) and continued his education in Germany, Switzerland, and Great Britain. Karski then entered the Polish diplomatic service. He was mobilized in 1939, taken prisoner by the Red Army, and sent to a Russian camp. He quickly escaped, returned to Nazi-occupied Poland, and joined the underground resistance movement. Because of his knowledge of languages he was used as a courier, making several trips between France, Great Britain, and his homeland. In 1940, he was captured by the Nazis but was rescued by the Polish Underground and was later sent to meet with high-level figures, including Anthony Eden and President Franklin Roosevelt.

After the war he refused to return to Poland and became an American citizen. He received his Ph.D. from Georgetown University. On several occasions he was sent by the State Department on lecture tours speaking in sixteen nations. Dr. Karski's book *Story of a Secret State* (1944) was a Book-of-the-

Month Club selection. His major work appeared in 1984: *The Great Powers and Poland, 1919-1945 (From Versailles to Yalta)*. He was awarded Poland's highest military decoration, several honorary degrees, and many tributes for his life's work.

HJC   What role did you play in alerting the West to the true nature of what was happening to Jews under Nazi occupation in Poland?

JK   In the summer of 1942, Mr. Cyril Ratajski, a delegate from the Polish government in exile, approved a request that I be sent on a secret mission to London as a courier for himself and for the leaders of the political parties organized in the Central Political Committee. This was to be my fourth secret trip between Warsaw, Paris, and London.

HJC   You were active in this work even though you had once been captured and tortured by the Nazis.

JK   The Gestapo arrested me and they beat me and beat me and beat me. I couldn't stand it. So I took a blade that I had hidden under the sole of my shoe and I cut my wrists. I was afraid they could make me talk and I knew all kinds of important information. I was taken to a hospital because I was in very bad shape and the Nazis wanted to keep me alive, to extract the facts from me. I was placed in a room with a guard outside the door. The Polish doctor who was taking care of me, while changing my bandages, whispered in my ear: "You must be sick, be very, very sick. We want to keep you here as long as possible." From that moment I simulated that I was dying. Some time later I conceived a plan. I pretended that since I was dying I had to go to confession. I said that as a Catholic who tried to commit a suicide which may still be successful I faced eternal hell. One of the hospital nuns got permission for me from the guard.

I was wheeled into the chapel and confessed to a Polish priest. Then I whispered to him a woman's name and address. "Someone must go to her," I explained. I used my pseudonym, Witold. The priest began to cry. He said, "People looking for sanctuary are abusing the Church. You cannot use confession for such a purpose." But then he asked me her

name and address. Two or three days later this woman came
to my room dressed in a nun's habit. I told her of my fear of
going back to the Gestapo and warned that I must either be
saved or be given poison. In a couple of days she returned with
some apples and hid some cyanide under my pillow. She told
me to take it only under extreme circumstances and that
they would attempt to save me. Jozef Cyrankiewicz, the
leader of the Socialist Underground in Cracow, organized my
escape. I was to take off my hospital clothes. When the doctor
entered the room with a cigarette, that was my signal to go to
the window which was above a flower bed and jump. Naked I
jumped, and two husky men were below. They caught me,
took me to a little boat on some river, and then to a little
estate whose owner at that time was Major Lucian Slawik. I
remained there for about four or five months. That was a
pattern that the underground had developed because they
could not trust escapees. Perhaps the Gestapo let them go
using them as spies.

HJC   Back to 1942—Jewish leaders contacted you about
your mission?

JK   Yes, members of the Socialist Bund and the Zionists
learned about it and gained permission to use my services in
order to communicate with their people in London and also
with the Polish government in exile as well as other Allied
authorities. I was not told the names of these two men, of
course, and this was proper procedure. Most postwar literature identifies them as Leon Feiner (Bundist) and Adolf
Berman (Zionist)—although Walter Laquer, in his book *The
Terrible Secret*, suggests that the Zionist representative may
have been Menachem Kirschenbaum. Others say it was Arie
Wilner.

Basically, the message given me to relay was as follows:
"The massacre of Jews was not motivated by German military requirements. Hitler and his accomplices decided on a
total annihilation of Jews regardless of the outcome of the
war. Jews in Poland are helpless. They cannot rely on the
Polish Underground or the general population. Some individuals are being saved but only the Allied governments can

effectively help. Historically, responsibility will rest on the Polish and the Allied governments if they fail to undertake appropriate measures."

HJC A number of concrete steps were offered, were they not?

JK I will mention the major ones exactly as I did at the International Liberators' Conference in Washington in 1981, of which you were a part. First, a public announcement that prevention of the physical extermination of the Jews become a part of the overall Allied war strategy, at the same time informing the German nation through radio, air-dropped leaflets, and other means about their government's crimes committed against the Jews.

Secondly, available data on the Jewish ghettos, concentration and extermination camps, names of the German officials directly involved in the crimes, statistics, facts and methods used should be spelled out. And public and formal demand for evidence that such a pressure has been exercised and Nazi practices directed against the Jews stopped.

Third, public and formal appeals to the German people to exercise pressure on their government to make it stop the exterminations.

Fourth, placing the responsibility on the German nation as a whole if they fail to respond and if the extermination continues.

Fifth, public and formal announcement that, in view of the unprecedented Nazi crimes against the Jews and in hope that those crimes would stop, the Allied governments were to take unprecedented steps.

HJC You mentioned other steps at the Liberators' Conference as well.

JK I did. These included the action of bombing special objects in Germany in retaliation for crimes committed against the Jewish people. German civilians would be warned ahead of time and told specifically that these attacks were a direct response to the attempted genocide of the Jews. Next, German prisoners of war would be apprised of these crimes directed towards Jews. Any of these prisoners who continued to profess solidarity with the Nazis would he held responsible. The same would be true of German nationals living in Allied countries. Finally, Jewish leaders in London, particularly Szmul Zygelbojm and Ignace Swarcbard, were solemnly urged to spare no effort in pressing the Polish government in exile to forward these demands to the Allied officials.

HJC Will you say something about your representation to the president of the Polish Republic, Wladyslaw Raczkiewicz?

JK My message to him was that many who persecuted Jews claimed to be Catholic. Religious sanctions from the Vatican, including excommunication, are within the Pope's jurisdiction, and statements from the Pope might have a strong impact on the German people. Hitler was a baptized Catholic and possibly he too might thus be made to reflect. I was ordered to deliver this message to President Raczkiewicz only. Otherwise it might become counterproductive in the hands of certain Jewish leaders.

The message I was to deliver to the prime minister and commander-in-chief, General Wladyslaw Sikorski, to Stanislaw Mikolajczyk, the minister of interior, and to Zygelbojm and Swarcbard was quite different. I was to tell them that while the Polish people in general were sympathetic to the problems of Jews, many Polish criminals rob, blackmail, denounce or even murder Jews in hiding. The Underground authorities must apply punitive measures against them, including executions—which must be publicized in the Underground press as a warning to others.

HJC As I understand it, you carried a specific message to Allied leaders as well as international Jewish leaders.

JK Correct. Much of it was an urgent appeal for funds. Gestapo leaders at every level were corruptible. Some Jews could buy their way out of Poland. Forged passports, accompanied by bribe money, would be useful. Allied countries must pledge sanctuary for the fleeing Jews. Money should be made available to Christian families in Poland which hide Jews because these families themselves are living at a low level of subsistence.

HJC You had two meetings with the Jewish leaders in Poland before you embarked on your mission to London. Was it not at the second encounter that they asked you to undertake further, extraordinary risks?

JK They feared that my report would seem too incredible and a result of hearsay. They thought it would be greatly enhanced if I came to the Allies as one who had witnessed what he talked about. They claimed contacts, even with Gestapo members, and asked me if I would allow myself to be smuggled into both the Warsaw Ghetto and the Belzec concentration camp.

HJC How did you react to such an invitation?

JK I agreed immediately. I didn't even think about it at the time. With the atmosphere that prevailed in Poland, with my previous missions, my background, I was an automaton. I did what I was asked to do. I gave it no thought. So I visited the [Warsaw] Ghetto two times in October of 1942, and a brief time after that I was smuggled into and out of Belzec. Two or three days later I began my secret trip to London. In November, I began reporting in London. I want to emphasize that my Jewish messages were only a portion of my overall assignment, but here I will confine myself to that part of my mission.

From November 1942 until June 1943 I was in personal contact with a great many important persons. I will name some of them: among the Poles were the previously mentioned Zygelbojm and Szwarcbard along with the Socialist Grosfeld and the liaison to Cardinal Hland (who at that time was living in the Vatican), Monsignor Kaczynski. There were four members of the British War Cabinet: Foreign Secretary Anthony Eden; Hugh Dalton, president of the Board of Trade; Arthur Greenwood, Labor party; and Lord Cranborne, Conservative party. There were others as well: Lord Selbourne of the War Office, European Underground Resistance; Ellen Wilkinson, a Labour Parliament member; Anthony Biddle, American ambassador to the Polish government; and such nongovernment persons as H.G. Wells, Arthur Koestler, and journalists, editors, publishers from various influential periodicals.

HJC   Can you point to any results that may have been caused by your discussion with these men and women?

JK   I cannot say that I alone am responsible—there were other reports as well. But let me mention some positive actions. Two weeks after I began my reporting, the Polish National Council passed a resolution condemning the murder of Jews and committed the government to move immediately. That was on December 7. On the tenth, the Polish government formally appealed to the Allied governments concerning the plight of Jews in Poland. Exactly one week after that the Allied Council, made up of representatives of all of the Allied governments, unanimously passed a public appeal on the situation. On December 19, President Raczkiewicz sent a communique to Pope Pius XII asking his intervention on behalf of the Jews. One month later, Poland's foreign minister, Edward Raczynski, presented his government's demand on behalf of Polish Jews at the Allied Nations' Council, asking for many of the actions I mentioned earlier. He did not ask for reprisals against German war prisoners or German nationals living in Allied nations. He considered such demands as contrary to the acceptable practices of international relations. All of Raczynski's demands were rejected by Anthony Eden, who merely offered vague promises to intervene in some neutral countries.

HJC   You did tell me once that your talk with Eden did not please you.

JK   I had admired Anthony Eden very much. For me he was the epitome of the career government official—competent, dignified, intelligent. But my opinion changed when I found him very abrupt and unwilling to discuss the problem of the Jews in Poland. He refused to hear me on this subject. In spite of this major obstacle, many articles based on my information began to appear in the British press early in 1943. Public demonstrations were organized. A pamphlet titled "The Fate of the Jews," co-authored by Thomas Mann, Alexey Tolstoy, and myself, was published in May.

HJC   How long was it until you went to Washington?

JK   I went in June of 1943, at the suggestion of Ambassador Biddle, and remained there until August.

HJC   You met with President Roosevelt.

JK   After having been told I would have twenty minutes with him, our meeting lasted an hour and twenty minutes. I did not notice that Roosevelt was ill, weak. The impression he made was as master of the world. The impression that he conveyed was that he didn't deal with people, with countries, with Poland—he dealt with the human race. He would arrange, finally, order in the world after the war. He made this kind of an impression on me. Then the Jewish problem. Yes, he did ask me questions—I answered those questions. And then I caught him in a trap. Roosevelt's secretary opened the door, for the second time, "Mr. President, people are waiting for you." I realized that the meeting was coming to the end. So I got up and then said to him: "Mr. President, I am going back to Poland, everybody will know I saw President Roosevelt. Everybody will ask me, 'What did the President tell you?' Mr. President what am I going to tell them?" You never forget this kind of a thing. He was smoking his cigarette and said, "You will tell your leaders that we shall win this war! You will tell them that the guilty ones will be punished for their crimes." Smoking, smoking. "Justice, freedom will prevail. You will tell your nation that they have a friend in this house. This is what you will tell them." At that time hearing from Roosevelt, "Your nation has a friend in this house," I was convinced that I heard the voice of almighty God. I settled all problems. I, Jan Karski, made the president a friend of my country. That was my impression. Only when I then walked to the car with the Polish ambassador who accompanied me he said, "Well, the president did not say much." He was clever. About the dead Jews, Roosevelt said nothing. So I was disappointed after all.

HJC   I know that on a second visit to this nation, beginning late in 1943, you gave some two hundred lectures and wrote a number of articles in leading magazines and newspapers, then published your book *Story of a Secret State*, a

Book-of-the-Month Club selection. But did you speak directly with other prominent Americans as you did with British figures?

JK   Yes, indeed. I will name some: Secretary of State Cordell Hull; Secretary of War Henry Stimson; Attorney General Francis Biddle; Archbishop Spellman; Cardinal Cicognani, the Apostolic Delegate; Dr. Nahum Goldman, president of the American Jewish Congress; Supreme Court Justice Felix Frankfurter; Rabbi Stephen Wise, who headed the World Jewish Congress, etc. I spoke with many prominent journalists including Walter Lippmann, Dorothy Thompson, William Prescott, and others.

HJC   Why did you not return to Poland?

JK   Prime Minister Mikolajczyk told me that it was too risky. The German radio had mentioned my activities in America and I was too easily identifiable by the scars on my wrists when I tried to commit suicide. It was decided that I had become too public a figure.

I take the editor's privilege at this point and append to this interview Dr. Karski's closing remarks at the Liberators' Conference alluded to in this interview.

Many of you at this conference gave testimony on the Jewish Gehenna. Respect is due to you. The Lord assigned me a role to speak and write during the war, when—as it seemed to me—it might help. It did not.

For me today, October 28, 1981, the curtain is down. The theatre is empty.

Furthermore, when the war came to its end, I learned that the government, the leaders, the scholars, the writers did not know what had been happening to the Jews. They were taken by surprise. The murder of six million innocents was a secret, a "terrible secret," as Laquer reports.

Then, I became a Jew. Like the family of my wife, who is sitting in this audience—all of them perished in the ghettos, in the concentration camps, in the gas chambers—so all murdered Jews became my family.

But I am a Christian Jew. I am a practicing Catholic. And, although not a heretic, still my faith tells me: the second Original Sin had been committed by humanity: through commission, or omission, or self-imposed ignorance, or insensitivity, or self-interest, or hypocrisy, or heartless rationalization.

This sin will haunt humanity to the end of time.

It does haunt me. And I want it to be so.

MARION PRITCHARD

In 1983, Marion P. van Binsbergen Pritchard was honored at Yad Vashem for her heroism in saving Jews from Nazi persecution in Holland.

After witnessing the public abuse of Jewish children by Nazis, Pritchard, six other young Christians, and two Jewish students organized themselves in resistance to such Nazi atrocities. After obtaining Aryan identity cards for their Jewish collaborators, the group located hiding places to assist escaping Jewish families and provided food, ration cards, and clothing where they could, while trying to give relief and moral support to host families who were risking their lives to care for strangers. They also helped to register newborn Jewish babies as gentiles. At a certain point Ms. Pritchard herself protected a family and shot a policeman who discovered their hiding place.

After the Second World War she worked to aid survivors in displaced persons camps in Germany, where she met the American who was to become her husband, Anton, who was working in a similar capacity. They later came to the United States, where she became a practicing pyschoanalyst. Her story appears in the film *The Courage to Care,* and she has been honored for her work by the Anti-Defamation League in the United States.

HJC   Where were you educated?

MP   I went to elementary school in Amsterdam, boarding school in England for a few years (the same boarding school my mother and my grandmother went to), then I went to Amsterdam for classical high school.

HJC   One of my areas of work used to be in English as a Foreign Language and I don't detect any accent in your speech.

MP   I was in a very fortunate position. My father was Dutch so he spoke Dutch to me; my mother was English and spoke only English. She did not learn Dutch until later. I had a French governess and we had German maids; everybody had German maids in those day. They worked for nothing. We grew up either tri-lingually or quadri-lingually because we learned the languages as we learned to talk. That has nothing to do with IQ.

HJC   Was there a specific problem with German maids when the war broke out?

MP   Germany was in a bad economic situation, especially after 1929. Even before that a lot of people in Holland had German maids.

HJC   Right. And so were they there when the war broke out?

MP   I guess some of them were. We had one Dutch and one Austrian maid. The latter was about twenty-four and hadn't been home in three years. My father insisted that she should go visit her family. He paid her fare back to Austria and she couldn't come back.

HJC   And your religious background is Anglican?

MP   Through my mother.

HJC   You are one of how many children?

MP   Two. I have a brother who is ten years younger than I am.

HJC   Now you're a practicing psychoanalyst in Vermont with three sons. How did you come to this country?

MP   When the war was over I went and worked in Jewish displaced persons camps in Germany. I wouldn't work in the others. That is where I met and married my American husband, who was among the first troops to enter Buchenwald. We worked in the DP camps for about two years, and then Anton decided that he needed a college education—which he hadn't gotten because his father lost his business in the economic crash. So we came here in 1947. He went to Harvard, finishing in three years—summa cum laude, Phi Beta Kappa. I'm very proud of him.

HJC   In what area?

MP   Social Relations. We found an apartment in Cambridge. I needed a job, so I applied with the Jewish Family and Children Service because they were responsible for the Jews who came from Germany to the United States. Most of them, of course, wanted to go to Israel. But those who came to the United States where being taken care of by the Jewish Family and Children Service in Boston. And I thought that was a good job for me because those people didn't have to tell me what they had been through. I knew. I was there. So they interviewed me and they said that their policy was not to hire Gentiles, so I went to work for the New England Medical Center instead. A year later, the Jewish Family and Children Service called me and asked if I were still interested in the job. I asked what happened to the philosophy. They said, "Our social workers all have master's [and] Ph.D. degrees, but they can't speak Yiddish and it is very hard to do case work through an interpreter." So I got to be a sort of reverse "shabbas goy" around there.

HJC   Do you speak Yiddish?

MP   Well, I learned in the DP camps and I spoke it fluently. My husband did too, and he's not Jewish either. I've lost a lot of it now. I can't speak it but I can understand it; I haven't had any practice lately.

HJC   Did these people that you were seeking employment from know your story?

MP   Oh, no. I never told anybody. Well, my husband knew a little bit because I loved being in touch with some of the people that I was involved with. But my children didn't know anything about it until the Israeli counsel in Boston invited them to come to the presentation of the medal.

HJC   And what year was that?

MP   1982.

HJC   You children didn't know until '82?!

MP   No.

HJC   Wow. Tell me why you went to work in a DP camp and why specifically that kind of camp?

MP   By the time the war was over I had gotten very attached to the three children that I had taken care of on a twenty-four hour a day basis for three years. The youngest was a week old when I got them. When the war was over she was two and a half. The family was about to be reunited, which was extremely fortunate, and I wanted to get away from that—and I didn't want to go to a regular job. I'd never been boxed up in one country before for five years. I thought it would be the quickest way to possibly find some of my Dutch-Jewish friends that I had totally lost track of, and I thought that if I were in Germany and worked in the DP camps I might meet them.

HJC   Is this correct? You knew the father of the three children you protected, but not the mother?

MP   Yes.

HJC   And they were reunited?

MP   Yes. She had a difficult time. She was half Jewish and very brilliant; sensitive but a deeply emotionally disturbed woman. At one point she had gotten furious with her husband because if he hadn't been "a god-damned Jew" her children wouldn't be at risk. She disappeared for the rest of the war. She came back after the war.

HJC   Do you think she was hiding?

MP   Well, she was hiding but she was also working with the Resistance. She is one of the only people I know—her Alzheimer's disease was diagnosd in the sixties and she is still alive. Her husband died last year in Holland.

HJC   You were in high school when the war broke out— is that correct?

MP   No, I was in the School of Social Work. I had been accepted in the school, but you have to be nineteen to be allowed to go. Holland has no colleges. You go straight from a

kind of high school that meets the university; you go straight
from a high school to law school, medical school, to social
work [school] or whatever. I was going to do a year's volunteer
work, six months in England and six months in Switzerland.
So I was in England when the war broke out between Germany and England. I wanted to stay, but my parents thought
(just like all Dutch people) that Holland would stay neutral
as it had in World War I. So I left on one of the last passenger
planes that went from England to Holland and spent the year
doing volunteer work in Holland before I ever entered the
School of Social Work. So the war broke out in May, which
was about four months before I started school.

HJC   I gather you knew Jewish people as part of your
regular group of friends.

MP   It is an interesting way to put it because I knew that
some of them were Jewish because they went to religious
instruction on Saturdays just like I knew some kids were
Catholic because they went to religious instruction after
school. I went on Sunday mornings. When the war broke out I
found out that some people I had been friends with for years
were Jewish and I didn't know it.

HJC   What moved you to become so deeply involved in
helping Jews specifically? Was there a particular incident?

MP   In a school of social work people in general are more
involved with whatever you call it—social justice—than
people who go to hairdresser's school, business school, or
whatever. There were Jews in the student body and a lot of
Jews on the faculty. As the anti-Semitic measures became
worse and worse, we talked with our friends and our faculty
members about what should be done. So it was a very gradual
process. I think that the real, absolute, furious, enraged commitment came the morning that I was on my way to the
school and they were emptying out a Jewish children's home.
These kids ranged in age from two to ten. It was a beautiful
spring morning, and it was a street I had known since I had
been born, and all of a sudden you see little kids picked up by
their pigtails or by a leg and thrown over the side of a truck—
into the truck. You stop but you can't believe it. Two women

came from the other side and they attacked the soldiers and tried to stop them and they got thrown on top of the kids. I know that was the moment I decided—

HJC Do you remember what your first specific activity was?

MP You mean in terms of that day or—?

HJC No, of assisting people who needed help.

MP No, because we had already started persuading people to hide. Trying to persuade them to hide was often very difficult.

HJC You were involved in helping get Aryan identification cards, finding hiding places?

MP Finding hiding places, trying to get relief. There was a very high official appointed by the Nazi occupation by the name of Hans Calmeyer. His job was, when Jews wanted to— there were all these exemptions that Jews could get. For instance, there was a period when any male Jew married to a non-Jew (I think it was that precise) if he agreed to be sterilized, wouldn't have to go to a concentration camp. Or if you worked for the Germans. Or if you could prove that you had been baptized as a Christian. And all those cases were decided upon by Calmeyer. Calmeyer did his damndest to help everybody he possibly could. And how he got away with it, I'll never know. I heard that he died because he became severely depressed in the seventies. I remember going to see him, and he told me that if I would go to the burgermeister of a town in the western part of Holland, and if the minister there had remembered having baptized the child, and if he had lost the particular page of the register, if he would give me a piece of paper that said he remembered baptizing this child, Calmeyer would give me the exemption. I did. I went there and came back and gave him the paper and he gave me the exemption. There were lots of things like that.

There were lists that you could get on by giving money and jewelry because, of course, the Germans' obsession was for getting everything from the Jews that they could. In trying to make sure that the Jews didn't give their diamonds or their other valuables to other people they made it possible for the

Jews to buy themselves onto the lists for money or whatever, of course, never planning to honor those lists. My father— I'm not an intellectual or a great thinker—but my father knew from the beginning that the Nazis were only doing that to get what they wanted. He told me that we were wasting our time and that the only possible way to help was to get Jews into hiding. And, of course, people didn't want to believe that.

HJC You mentioned a clergyman who was willing to remember the baptism. Did you find that was the general pattern or did you find they hesitated to cooperate in telling a lie to save a life?

MP I didn't ask that many. If I had asked a hundred I could say to that, twenty did and eighty didn't, or something like that. But I wasn't conducting research at the time.

HJC What was the tone, the atmosphere in Holland?

MP It was very different from one place to another. I spent very little time in the south of Holland. As far as I know, in the south, where the Catholics are the strongest, the Catholic people and the Catholic priests were very good in cooperating and hiding Jewish children and not trying to turn them into little Catholics. There are sections of Holland where there were very few Jews to begin with, and the issue didn't come up. Amsterdam was heavily Jewish. There is a relatively large Jewish population in Amsterdam. I can't compare, and I can't say how many, but when I hid that man and his three children—the movie sort of makes it look like I did it all by myself. We lived in the back part of this house that I had known all of my life. The woman who owned it was a friend of my parents, she was in her seventies then, and I asked if I could live there. Her son-in-law, who had gone to the university with the Jewish man, asked me if I would take care of the Jew, and he arranged that we would live in the back part of his mother-in-law's house. She never asked who these kids were, and I had known her all my life. There was a farmer nearby whom I had also known since I was born, and he brought me a quart of milk every day. On the black market he could have gotten a fortune for a quart of milk the last year of the war; it was certainly very strongly against the German law to provide food for Jewish children. He knew what I was doing. The undertaker who helped me bury the corpse of the man I killed—he knew what I was doing. They all knew. They all helped. Everybody knew this policeman killed.

HJC I'll come back to that shortly. You moved from your parents' home to accommodate this family.

MP My father died in '42. I think that he developed cancer, that there was a psychosomatic reaction to the German occupation. My father's family studied law as far back as there were law schools in Holland. The women went to law school, too. Very few of them ever practiced but everybody went. I mean *justice*, not law and order. My father said to me that I didn't have to go, and he was going to say the same to my brother. But he was a great believer in justice. He was very disgusted with the Dutch government that equivocated before the war about allowing Jews to enter from Germany to Holland freely. And, of course, when the Germans moved in, the Dutch justice and the whole Dutch judicial system and philosophy went out the window and Nazi doctrine became the law. He couldn't tolerate that. And the Germans came to get him. What the Germans used to do was take prominent people hostage, and when the Resistance did something the Germans didn't like they would take out five or ten or twenty and make people watch while they shot them. When they came to get my father to take him hostage he was so ill already that they decided that he wasn't worth taking.

HJC So after he died you left? You were asked to take care of . . .

MP No, I had another year in the School of Social Work at that time. It was early in 1943 that I started taking care of Freddie and the kids full time.

HJC Were you not working then? You were, in a sense, mothering?

MP I graduated from the School of Social Work—oh, I think I do remember the first—I'll come back to that in a second. I had started—they had asked me earlier, in September or October, if I could take care of them. I didn't know them. I said, "Look, I've got to finish school, but then I'll do it." And I started going out there weekends to get to know the kids. But while I was still at the School of Social Work, I was doing—we had to do field work on Saturdays in settlement houses and I was working in a so-called "antisocial" village in Amsterdam. (It's a village where antisocial families were made to live under a village supervisor.) A woman ran a day-care center where the ones who had abused their children had to bring their children there during the daytime. And they were encouraged to stay themselves and help take care of the kids. They tried to help the fathers get jobs while the kids went to school and all that. So I worked there on Saturdays with some other students, and there was one Jewish family there. The head of that antisocial village asked me to take this little boy home. That was the first time I was physically, actively involved with such activity.

HJC   And the person who asked you to help this child knew that you would be at risk doing that?

MP   Oh yes. She was at risk for not having thrown them out of the village.

HJC   We got into this by my asking if you mothered the children full-time. You did not have a job.

MP   No.

HJC   How did you hide the family?

MP   The living room had a window. There was a table that stuck out from under the window with two small benches on either side and a rug underneath. The son-in-law and his brother dug a hole underneath—big enough for the man to be in and the children. I didn't always put the children in. Kids under six didn't have to wear the yellow stars. I'm sure the neighbors had questions about these kids, but I let them play outside in the garden. But, at night, if we knew that there was a raid coming, we did put them in there.

HJC   In the hole?

MP   Yes. At night we moved the benches aside. We moved the table aside. We opened up the hole. From the place where a truck would have to stop, to the front door of the house, would take at least, in the dark at night, at least a couple of minutes. So, we practiced and practiced. I could get them in that hole and the entire thing covered up in about seventeen seconds.

HJC   With no guarantee, of course, that the children, the youngest ones, would be quiet.

MP   Well, the two older knew enough to be quiet. The baby I had sleeping powders for.

HJC   Is that right? Did you ever have to use that?

MP   Yes. You never knew if you were going to have to or not, so you played it safe.

HJC   So you did use the sleeping powder a few times?

MP   Yes. The night that we got caught. . . . What the Germans often did was come and search, and if they didn't find anything and they suspected that you were hiding somebody, they learned to come back half an hour, or an hour, or an hour and a half later—figuring that the people would relax. And, of course, at first, when they did that, it worked. These were all things that you learned. The Germans do something, you react, they react, you react, they react. But the reason I brought the kids out was because the baby began to cry. So I got the kids out. I put the two boys to bed in the other room and I was trying to calm the baby down when this one—the Dutch policeman—came back.

HJC   What risk were you at doing this? Imprisonment? Concentration camp?

MP   Well, of course every day there were new edicts and orders etc., etc. And the official order was that if you were caught helping Jews, you would suffer their fate. You might be locked up, sent to a concentration camp, killed—whatever. What happened in practice was as seemingly arbitrary as a whole lot of things that the Germans did. I know people who were hiding somebody, the Germans came, they found the people they were hiding, and they never came back. They went scot-free. There was a woman at the Faith of Human-kind Conference in Washington, a Dutch woman, whose husband and children were taken—her husband was beaten and killed. They beat up her children. Other people were sent to concentration camps. You just never knew.

HJC   Do you remember the date when this specific incident occurred?

MP   1944.

HJC   Tell what happened that night.

MP   We were all in bed and asleep. I always woke up when there was a truck or a car, because trucks or cars could only be bad news. There was a curfew for ordinary people. Besides, ordinary people didn't have trucks or cars anymore. So I got everybody into the hiding place. We kept the sleeping powders and some water down there, so the father could give it to the baby girl after they were down there, to save time. The authorities came in, they searched the place, they yelled and screamed, and I insisted that I was all alone there. I know that lots of people did this, if the Germans came at night and they walked into a house when everybody is in bed. If there are five people in the house, there should be five pillows and five messed up beds, or four messed up regular beds and one double bed, or whatever. So what we did was have the people who were in hiding sleep with the people who were hiding them. (And that created some interesting situations.) But anyway, we only had one visible bed, the kids' beds were all made up. So they looked and they looked, and they didn't find anything, and they left, and then the Dutch policeman came back.

HJC   How long later?

MP   Say, about an hour, an hour and a half. And I had a gun, that a friend had given me, which I absolutely never, ever intended to use. I had done some hunting as a child in England but that was the limit of my interest in bearing arms.

HJC   And this was a pistol?

MP   Yes, very small.

HJC   And why did he give it to you?

MP   He thought I might need it.

HJC   He gave it to you how long before that, roughly?

MP   As soon as I moved in.

HJC   Which was what—a year before?

MP   Something like that.

HJC   And the gun was loaded? But you never cleaned it or anything?

MP   I had it on a bookshelf above the bed.

HJC   Ready to go if you needed it and yet, you were certainly going to be hesitant about using it?

MP   When I first had it, I was terribly conscious of it in terms of worrying that the boys would find it and play with it. And then, as I got used to it being there, and so many things happened—every day there was some other crisis—I sort of forgot it was there for the longest time. But at the right time I knew it was there.

HJC   So what happened? The policeman drove back in a car?

MP   I didn't hear a car. I didn't hear anything. He knew the area very well and he probably walked.

HJC   What did he do—knock on the door or walk in or what?

MP   He banged on the door. I opened it up.

HJC   And what did he say? Do you remember?

MP   Well, I hadn't put the hiding place back together again. I put it back together, but not properly. And I saw him going for it and I didn't wait.

HJC   So you went right for the pistol.

MP   Yes.

HJC   Was he facing you? Did he have his back to you?

MP   He was facing me. He went and looked at the area and he could tell where the seams in the linoleum were and he looked back at me and he looked back triumphant. And while he had his back to me, I'd gone and gotten the pistol. I didn't want to shoot because I was afraid I'd scare the baby— ridiculous, right? But those are the thoughts that go through your head. So then when he turned around and looked at me I did it. I'm not proud of it.

HJC   Did he realize what was happening to him? Was there a moment . . . ?

MP   Funny. There's a moment of tremendous elation— but no more than a split second.

HJC   And then how did you dispose of him?

MP   I knew somebody who lived next door and I sent him to get the butcher from the village, who I knew would help.

HJC   This is the middle of the night?

MP   About three o'clock in the morning. The butcher came and I didn't have to tell him anything, he could see. So he went and got the undertaker who came and got the body and they moved it in a bread wagon. The baker used to drive around with a horse and wagon, so they put the body in there, took it to the funeral home, and he put it in a coffin . . . with another corpse and didn't tell the family. They had the funeral that afternoon or the next day or whenever. I just hope that the family would have approved.

HJC   You mentioned to me, once on the phone, that if somebody really wanted to find out what happened to this police officer, they probably could have. But the cover-up was . . .

MP   Everybody hated him. They hated him before the war. He was just a—he'd become a Nazi. You know, the Dutch had a Nazi party before the war. It was a small percentage of the population that joined. I'm sure that the Dutch Nazi party was the only one that accepted Jews. It had Jewish members—until the invasion, when the occupying Germans made the Dutch Nazis throw out Jews. If anybody had really wanted to find out, they could have.

HJC   Now after that, you were imprisoned? Or you were arrested, at least for a while?

MP   That was long before that.

HJC   Oh, it was before that you were arrested?

MP   It had nothing to do with my Jewish activity.

HJC   You were picked up with a group of about forty people?

MP   No, there weren't that many. That was in my second year at the School of Social Work. In order to study with your friends you had to spend the night, because there was a curfew. You had to be in by eight o'clock. So this particular night I was studying with some friends, students who were from outside of Amsterdam. The universities in Holland don't have housing. People rent apartments or houses together. So this girl and five or six other girls lived in this house. What they were doing was distributing—you were not allowed to listen to the Allied news, you weren't allowed to listen to the BBC or anything like that. Some people did listen to the BBC news and then reproduced it, not as sophisticated as now, but the 1940s variation of xeroxing.

HJC Mimeographing.

MP Mimeographing, right. And they distributed it to whoever wanted to read it. And they had been betrayed. So when the Nazis wanted to arrest people, they went at night most of the time, because they knew that people would be home. So they came that night and there were the five or six people who actually lived in the house. They picked them up and everybody else who was there.

HJC How long were you in prison?

MP They kept us for six months in the Amsterdam prison that my father was on the Board of Regents of. The Germans would take part of the prison for their purposes and leave part of it to the Dutch for their own petty criminals.

HJC In spite of that less-than-pleasant experience, you were willing to take the later risks that you took.

MP I think it made me all the more adamant.

HJC What was the experience the next time you were taken? That's with the group of about forty people.

MP Oh yes. The last winter of the war was known in Holland as "the Winter." Everybody was really starving to death. There was no food, there was no electricity, there was no water, there was nothing. And people in the western part of Holland, the industrial part, would go up to the northeast where the farmers were and beg, borrow, or steal food. If you were lucky, like I, you had some things you could trade— silver (I took my flute, I took some family silver, I forget what else). And I also knew some people up there. So I was in a very fortunate position. We went up there, got food, and then to come back you had to cross a river. And of course it was a good place for the Germans to check people, because the Germans by that time were starving to death themselves.

They would simply stop people and take what they had. You could get across. You could rent a boat. There were horror stories of our people who had rented a boat, and then the people who rented the boat [to them] would dump them over in the middle of the river and keep the food. It sounds awful, but when you're that desperate and that hungry, people do things that under normal circumstances they would never have done. So by the time I had got to that check point, the Germans had a big guard house there and there were always rumors on the road how this was not the time to go—it's safe to cross, it's not safe to cross. Sometimes they wouldn't bother people for two days, then there would be two days nobody could get across except if they were legal. So the rumor was it was okay to get across, and we started across, and then we got picked up and taken to this German guard house, and we were told that we would be released the next morning at the end of curfew time, but that everything that we had gotten would be confiscated. That was when I lost my temper. I told them what I thought of their leader and the Nazis. Totally out of control. And people were trying to stop me because I was saying such awful things—they thought that I and maybe they, too, might get shot on the spot. It was a possibility; you never knew with the Germans. But they didn't. And I finally sort of wound down and dozed until the next morning. Two German soldiers came in and they came straight for me and the woman next to me looked at me—she said, "Oh my God, now you're going to get it," and I thought I was, too. And they took me outside, they gave me back the bike, they gave me back the food, they put me on a truck and drove me across the river.

HJC Why?

MP Well, I used to like to think that I'd made an impression on them. And by then the troops that occupied the country were . . . the troops that came in first were the beautiful, six-foot tall, blond, blue-eyed, Hitler-educated and indoctrinated members of the Nazi race. By the end of the war, the occupying army consisted of children under sixteen—boys fourteen, fifteen, sixteen—and men in their forties, fifties, and sixties. My guess is that some of them couldn't have cared less. I like to think that these guys heard me and decided to show that all Germans were not that bad. It has been suggested to me that they knew that the end of the war was coming and they figured that if they did something like that, maybe later, when they were completely defeated, some Dutchman would speak up for them. I don't know. I didn't ask.

HJC I want to get back to the incident that was specifically related in *Courage to Care*, the shooting of the Dutch officer. The impression that this made on me was very Bonhoefferian. Dietrich Bonhoeffer, who, I think, probably since the war has been the most influential Christian theologian— in American seminaries, certainly—talked about the times being such that Christians could not live without getting their hands dirty. And this seemed to be—your act seemed to be a reflection of that. That you had to . . .

MP That's very well said. That makes me feel better. I feel very much two ways about it. I really don't believe in killing. Not at all. I don't believe in capital punishment. For no crime do I believe in capital punishment. I think there are people who should be locked up until the end of their days to protect other people. But capital punishment, I've been against,—unequivocally against it all my life. So that that act has bothered me. Still does.

HJC And yet, the situation was such, you felt you had to act.

MP To save my kids, and the father.

HJC It wasn't just him or you, obviously.

MP No.

HJC And in taking the children, you assumed a certain responsibility.

MP Yes.

HJC I think the prayer for most of us is, "Oh God, don't put me in such a position."

MP Yes.

HJC You faced it for some of us.

LEON WELLS

Dr. Leon Wells was taken by the Nazis from his native city of Lvov, Poland, in 1941 and interned in the Janowska concentration camp. He escaped but was recaptured and assigned to what was known as the "Death Brigade," reflecting his youth and relative good health. The Death Brigade was to obliterate evidence of the Nazi mass-murders when it became clear that Germany would lose the war. Part of Wells's task included helping to dig the mass graves to dispose of the bodies of victims in secretive ways. He escaped a second time and hid from his captors until liberation.

After earning his doctorate at the Technical University, Munich, in 1949, Wells did postgraduate study at Lehigh University. He became a physicist and inventor in the field of applied optics and mechanisms, receiving a number of patents on motion picture projection systems. His account of his experiences from 1941 to 1945 appears in *The Janowska Road* (1963) (later titled *The Death Brigade*). His volume *Who Speaks for the Vanquished?* (1987) raises serious, critical questions about the roles played by certain American Jewish leaders and organizations in dealing with victims of the Holocaust. Dr. Wells has also published a work not translated into English, *Mathematische Vorschule Fuer Ingenieure und Naturforscher* (1949), and has been published in the *New York*

Times, Reconstructionist, and other publications. He won the Industrial Motion Picture award in 1960.

HJC You tell in your book *The Janowska Road* about several members of your family being betrayed by neighbors and friends.

LW Yes.

HJC What does this make you feel about humanity?

LW It makes me feel bad, on one hand, and on the other hand, I was also hidden by complete strangers, Christians in Lvov who cared for twenty-three people in their basement. I had experience on both sides. So where do I stand? Do I speak about the Kalwinskis or do I speak about the betrayers? This is a continuous problem. Is the glass half-empty or do you speak about the half-full glass? I am a little disturbed by a basic problem. There were, according to Dr. Philip Friedman, 100,000 Poles who risked their lives to save complete strangers, of a different religion. I feel, maybe, if there would have been 500,000 instead of 100,000, good people like these 100,000, my family would have been saved. So let us for the future try to increase 100,000 to 500,000 instead of emphasizing the negative, the half-empty. Let us fill the glass.

So I am torn but I feel very strongly about it because I am alive, I have a beautiful family, and everything because of one good Christian family. And I would like to increase the number. Then we will live in a good world. If we don't increase it, it is kill or be killed, and that's not a solution for me. From a nationalistic viewpoint, a lot of people believe that the enemy is bad, kill him even before he raises his head. Kill him ahead of time. Don't think. He is officially bad. I don't want to add to that. So I speak more about the Kalwinskis, the people who saved me, than about our neighbors who gave out. And my own family said, why don't I speak more about those neighbors. That is already finished for me. There's no reason for me to live if this is only a terrible world. Let us try to improve it.

HJC The Kalwinskis, as I understand it, did this even when neighbors were caught doing this and were executed.

LW Not only these. Next to us a household was executed. Very few people analyzed the situation, what it meant
to save somebody and risk their lives. Last week in Washington, a person from Yad Vashem was telling about the
people in Holland. If they were caught hiding Jews, they were
sent to a concentration camp. There was a 90 percent chance
that they would survive the war. In Poland, the Polish people
being looked down on by the Germans, if they were caught,
were executed immediately. It was a different situation in
Poland than in Holland. Practically the only countries under
German occupation that did not have a Quisling government
were Poland and Holland. All other countries had a Quisling
government. And in all the other countries where there were
Quisling governments cooperating with the Nazis, the Jews
survived in bigger numbers. A lot of people don't want to hear
about facism, like in Italy. I do not like fascism but it did
much less harm than Nazism. Even Denmark had a collaboration government. In Poland I was a witness; I'm the only
one left because I was in the Death Brigade.

In 1941 the Germans called the leading Polish intelligent-
sia of leadership potential (professors and others who were
involved in politics), and they offered them to create a government under Hitler. The Poles refused. The Germans threatened to kill them. "You will not survive." and the Polishmen
answered, "We will take our death." I wish, as a Jew, that they
would have accepted the offer. Because we would have had
the same problem as under [Miklos] Horthy. We escaped to
Hungary, where Horthy cooperated with the Nazis. And I
personally, in the Death Brigade, was exhuming the bodies
and found them and became a witness in Poland. Because
they disappeared. The Nazis did not come and publicly say,
"We killed them." But they chose death instead of cooperation with the Nazis, and that was our tragedy. Exactly
opposite of what many think. Nobody wants to say that
sometimes cooperation with your enemy is the solution for
you, but this is the fact. Dr. Ostrowski, Professor Stozek, and
Professor Bartel, the whole thirty-eight people, the cream of
Poland's social and intellectual life, I have listed in *The Death*

Brigade. All of them were non-Jews who refused to cooperate with the Nazis in any way.

HJC   You were the only witness to much of this, weren't you?

LW   The first book published about the concentration camp, after the war, by the Polish Historical Commission, was mine. And I was the only witness that the leadership of Poland was killed. Because I helped to undig their bodies. Right after the war I gave evidence over to the Historical Commission in Lodz.

HJC   Jean Améry in his book *At the Mind's Limit* talks about what happens to one who is tortured. He writes that the intellect and the imagination don't count. The only reality is the flesh. He says a man who is once tortured is *always* tortured. Do you want to speak to that from your own experience?

LW   I speak from my own experience and also from people whom I know. Some of them are tortured and none of us, none of us, can get away from our own backgrounds. This became the most important part of our youth. Most of us were young. You *are* tortured. Some people solve it in different ways. Some people solve it by hate. Some people solve it by love. I am afraid to say—and I mentioned it last week on the radio—I came to Israel after the '67 war and asked a friend, how did you react? He was in the army. He had lost his wife and daughter in Auschwitz. He was in his late forties, early fifties. He fought for Israel. He said to me, "Leon, it made me feel great." And I asked, "Why?" He said "In Auschwitz when I laid on the floor and was being kicked by the SS man, I was saying to myself, I wish I could get up and kick him." Which is a normal reaction for anybody. "Now I was standing and kicking them." He did not any more see the SS men, he saw the world as enemies. And I feel to a certain degree, the hunted becomes the hunter. Or you have to escape another way. This is why I don't remember as much the half-empty glass as I would like to fill the half-full glass to fullness.

I had Mrs. Kalwinska in my house, seven, eight years ago.

She died since. I took her to church. I never went to church.
But she could not speak any English, only Polish. I had to
translate. It was difficult for her, you know, not to speak to
anybody. But I took her to church because I felt so close to her.
But unfortunately even these good people were somehow
punished. She lost her only daughter of twenty-four two
years after the war from a very mysterious sickness. A girl
that used to come to our basement and sit with us on Sunday.
I'd say to her that she should go out on Sunday, not to sit with
us in the basement. She said, "How can I enjoy myself if you
people sit in a basement and I go out and have a good time?"
She said, "It's torture." So she sat with us all day Sunday.
That was her day off. The other days she had to work. But
she died within two years after liberation, giving birth. The
brother is here in America. I brought him. So I have these
things in my memory. Marisha's not dead, because I cannot
believe it. The same as my family. But I cannot hate and go
out and kill people. And teach my children, too. I did not
survive because I was like the Nazis, a killer. But on the other
hand, a lot of us had this feeling: kill or be killed. That is the
only conclusion I feel people will arrive at today if we don't
teach properly about the Holocaust. We people of the Holocaust suffered. But today they say, what do I care about fifty
years ago? I remember in '35 or '36 I was only ten years old
and heard my father telling his friends about the First World
War that was only fifteen, sixteen years previous and I
thought, "Ah, again speaking about the old times." It looked
to me like really old things. Today we are speaking about
forty-five years ago. And we want the world to know, "Don't
you know, it happened to us!" It's us. It's not them.

The only way that I can talk to my children, and I hope that
they will survive and don't want another Holocaust or another war, is by looking at the half-full glass, at Mrs. Kalwinska. Do you know we have published books about the
survivors' children? We have a second generation of survivors. We don't have and never bothered about the second
generation of people that helped. Staszek tells me he was
eight years old. I know that he was the beloved son of his

mother. He was the youngest, the little one. One day, he
walked up to his mother and said, "Look, our electricity
meter is running. Who has lights during the day? We were in
the basement. The mother looked at him and decided the
next day that she had to send him away. Eight years old! A
kid! A baby! He said, "My mother sent me away to strangers.
About 400 kilometers from Lvov. She told me that I am
going away because I'm afraid of bombing by the Russians."
He said, "I liked bombing, I liked the excitement. But they
were telling me that I don't like it, that I am afraid. I told
them I was never afraid. They said you don't know it but
you're afraid." So they found a family that took in their
beloved son. They sent him 400 kilometers away so he
could not betray us accidentally. Another time Staszek's
brother ran in the fields one day with his friend, a Ukrain-
ian. And there were a Jewish boy and a girl escaping. They
came to the brother and said, "Help us! Help us! The Germans are after us." He said he got tears in his eyes but told
them, "I don't care to help you. I don't like Jews." He felt
that if he helped, his friend would not. Until today it haunts
him, he told me. He turned away two young kids because if
he had taken them in he would have skinned twenty-three
Jews, everybody would have known in five minutes that
they had Jews in the basement. He had to become a hater of
Jews to save us. He said, "It haunts me. Every night I see
these two kids." Nobody cares about these second-genera-
tion people who helped Jews. The eldest son was married.
He married a widow with two children. They did not have a
good marriage. The son was the same as Mr. Kalwinski, he
liked to have a drink. So the mother couldn't tell her son
that they hid Jews because if he had a drink he might talk
out. And the wife, being mad at him, could tell on him. So
they didn't tell the son that the father was hiding Jews. Not
because they were afraid, not because of any anti-Semitism,
but because it was a simple human thing: if he drinks and if
he has a problem with the wife. . . . People don't realize what
it meant to hide somebody, to sacrifice. I ask audiences
continuously, "How many of you would have risked your

lives to save a stranger?" I never knew where the Kalwinskis lived. I never knew their streets. I came through a fellow inmate who escaped with me from the Death Brigade. I never knew where I was. How many would risk your lives for a complete stranger?

HJC   And the lives of their children . . .

LW   The life of their whole family. So there was this one man down the street who had a fight with his sixteen-, seventeen-year-old daughter. And the daughter ran out in madness and yelled out, "You see, my father's holding Jews," to punish him. Next day the Jews and he and his wife were hanged in the middle of the street. But can you say that the daughter was anti-Semitic? How many of us have fights with our daughters, our children, teenagers, and they run out and say anything and afterwards they are sorry? How many times are we grownups sorry for what we have said? But here she jumped out, one word, and everyone was finished. Her father and mother were hanged on a tree.

Adam Kaufmann, who was a leading Polish socialist before the war, was telling me a story of hiding a Jew. (They called those hiding Jews in Poland crypto-Jews.) A Polish woman hid a Jew, also a woman. They had only one room; she was a poor servant. When somebody knocked at the door, this Jew would go into the closet to hide. The police came one night and the Jewish woman ran into the closet. The Pole had not covered her windows completely, so there was light coming through. And she said she would cover them and the police left. She went to the closet and called the Jew who did not come out. So the Polish woman started to look for the other one. She thought maybe she went to some other place. But then she found her in the closet where the Jew had a heart attack and died. The problem became how to get rid of the body, a Jewish body. She went down to the super and told him the whole story. The super said he would carry the corpse to the top of the house, hang her and say that a Jewish woman committed suicide in the middle of the night in our house. So they did it, they hanged her and it was thought that she committed suicide. In Poland, there is a belief that the rope of

a suicidal person brings you all the luck that you need in life.
Everybody in the street wanted a piece of the rope. So the
super thought that he could make some money. And he
started to sell pieces of rope. He sold fifteen or twenty pieces
and collected some money. With the money he went to the
neighborhood bar and got himself drunk. He laughed at the
people: "Look what they paid me money for. I hanged this
woman; she was a Jewish woman." I don't know the whole
story to the end.

But what I want to emphasize is the idea that hiding
somebody wasn't a simple thing only. The tragedy is that
history does not know them for very simple reasons. They
are such good people that they don't even think that they did
something terrific. So they don't advertise themselves. But if
it is not written in books, who will know about it? Nobody. It
will not remain in history. You cannot prove it; it becomes
bologna. But these people cannot say, "Look at me, I am a
hero, I saved Jews." No. And the others were not interested.
Israel had the problem, mainly, to educate a people from
Galot—from the diaspora—to military power. And Israel has
this problem, basically, to teach military power. Nobody
likes you; you see what happened to you in the Holocaust.
There is no room to tell about good people. You should tell
the truth, that somebody helped you, but don't emphasize it
and don't make it big. Make it the minimum. I tell people
that Poles saved Jews, that the biggest number among people
who saved Jews are Poles. They look at me, "Is this true?"
You see, people don't want to believe They say that Poles are
anti-Semitic and everybody knows it. You don't have to prove
a lot of things in life, just say everybody knows it and that's
enough. That's your proof!

HJC Let me ask you this: You had one of the most horrible assignments in the camps. You had to dig up bodies
and cremate them. How did you continue living? Charlotte
Delbo, in her book, said, "We came back from a day's work
and the first part of the conversation was, Who died today?
We'd find out who died and then we'd go back to the regular
conversation." She said, "My sister, somebody's sister, would

be killed while we were marching and we'd keep on marching." How do you do that?

LW   The instinct of survival is so great. I could do it easier
than some others because I was sixteen, seventeen years old.
And I believe youth helps because there's one direction. The
older people, even if they are only forty, fifty, they're older
people. Children can survive parents; parents cannot survive
children. That's the old philosophy that there's one direction
in life. This I remember from the Janowska camp, and the
same in the Death Brigade, that the people who are already
dead are lucky people because you have to be tortured longer
and die anyway. You will be killed too, because the whole
idea was that you would be killed. The only thing is that they
were killed before you—so they don't have a longer day. You
were not able to die—you have to be sophisticated to commit
suicide. If you look up the statistics you see that less poor
people commit suicide than rich people. It was known that
more German Jews and Austrian Jews committed suicide
than Polish Jews. You have to have a certain sophistica-
tion and a certain education to commit suicide. We never
thought, why do I need to wait for the Nazis to do it? Let me
jump first, let me kill myself. It was only the educated that
had a poison pill or something. The simple person thought,
I'll die when they kill me. There was no other way out of
these tortures and miseries.

You go out in the morning, get beaten, and you go back in
the evening and continue. We even had sex jokes and so on,
because we tried to be normal in an abnormal situation. As I
say at the end of my book *The Janowska Road,* one man who
lost his wife and children said, "What do I need to live for?"
When it came that he had a choice to escape and maybe even
a small chance that he would survive, he said, "What for?"
He did not live there to survive. He lived there to die. Afterwards, you make it out that you want to be a witness, but it's
only a shield, it's not a reality that this is why you live. But
you have to excuse yourself for living, so you say you want to
tell the world—and before you know you are also taking
revenge. Then after a while, you start your own life, you have

your own family, you have a different responsibility, which is also a certain amount of self-defense. If you have responsibility, you cannot give up. Not because you cannot do it, but you do not want to because the instinct of survival is greater than the instinct of death.

HJC   Having said that, if I understand correctly, at a certain point when you were outside of the Lvov ghetto, you voluntarily went back into the ghetto.

LW   Yes, that was where I belonged. It is like a man who is let out of jail and his life is only in the jail. You know, people don't understand the philosophy of people in jail. I feel a lot of that could be applied, but we became so emotional that we didn't want to speak about it. It's like in the old times, if your child were crippled, you didn't say anything negative or didn't touch him. He had enough problems. But then nobody learned from it. We don't want to speak about it because there was a feeling of guilt. There are some survivors that still feel guilty for having survived. They survived and all their family, their young children, brothers and sisters died and they went into hiding. To speak about the greatness of the hiding is like making yourself a hero, while the others died. So they did not think it such a wonderful thing. We always can find this half-empty, or little empty, or half-full, or little full glass. It depends what you are looking for, what you want from life. I feel, having three children, that my biggest responsibility is for them, for the future, and I don't see any future in "kill or be killed." How to stay alive. I don't believe in martyrdom. I don't believe in a good death or a bad death. I feel death is death. Suffering is suffering. It does not ennoble you.

HJC   After having seen all of this, are you a believer?

LW   I am not. I am completely a problematic person. I want and I don't want. I am mixed up and I don't very often face it. I read the Lubavitch in '43, '44—it's not proper to mention—Soloveitchik and all the others, they said the Holocaust was sent from heaven and did good because it is the time of the coming of the Messiah. Even the Lubavitch in '43, I have here the document where he said enjoy, enjoy, because the Messiah is coming. And he said that Haman does not come by himself. He's sent by God. I said to a major Jewish theologian recently, "Why are you only condemning the Pope? Or about what Cardinal O'Connor in New York said about the Holocaust?" I said, "Didn't the Lubavitch and others say the same, that it's God's will and we should believe it? It is only a cleansing, because of our sins. God threw us out from our land because of our sins." And he said, "Yes, if you are a religious man and if I would be the Pope, I couldn't behave differently because I cannot say it's not God's will because he can stop everything." I said, "Fine. So why don't you as a leading Jewish theologian come out and ask why are we jumping so much about the Pope and all?" He said, "What should I do? It is the people, it is their will. They know what they want to hear and I know what I want." And I said to myself, it is theological, they have no other choice. There is no other choice. If you believe in a God, then it's the will of God. We'd have to change the whole religious outlook in order to see it differently. But as of the moment, we believe in God's will.

I spoke at a Catholic college not long ago. They were very nice people, very fine people—and one said to me, "Aren't you happy that your parents died and now, like Jesus' disciples, are sitting next to God?" The Lubavitch said exactly the same, in '43, one month before the uprising in the Warsaw Ghetto. You have it in my book. Enjoy, enjoy, the Messiah's coming because he's cleaning up. How can I believe in such a God? So I have this mixed feeling and I don't want to face it. The best thing is never to face it.

HJC Let us shift from God to Man, if you will. Early in *The Janowska Road*, you say, "Every Jew, we were told, is responsible for all other Jews." In your new book *Who Speaks for the Vanquished?* that's the subject you take up: the responsibility of one Jew for another. And you mention in the introduction your gratitude to the editor, Michael Ryan, because you were very angry and he tempered this anger. Even so, there are some very angry parts in the book.

LW You know, you as a Christian say in the prayer every day, God, forgive my sins as I forgive my enemies.

HJC You memorized the catechism, you said.

LW I knew it all in Latin. This is a basic prayer. And not said once in a while, but every day. Every child in school in Poland had to say that prayer in the morning; it was a Christian custom. This does not mean that they do what they say. I myself from '45 to '60 went through a complete change. I wanted to believe. I wanted to differentiate myself from Christianity. I wanted to be the part of a winner. I was still in a basic contest. Who won, I or Hitler? Zionism told me a story too—that from now on you fight, you have your own country, and there will be no more holocausts, but if we acquiesce, then there will be another Holocaust. I wanted all of this so I expressed it at this time. Since '62, '63, when I started to study, I saw some of us like these people who say their prayers every day but don't adhere to them. So I started to study the background. Hadassah, the American Jewish Congress, and the World Jewish Congress spoke for me until I learned certain things. From all my studying I got wiser. Like Solomon said, you have to learn. But my emotions tell me that I wanted to belong to a club. As a young man, I wanted to be part of a different group. I never wanted to join the Nazis. One man, in the *New York Times*, said my biggest problem is that I wasn't accepted in the Brown Shirts. That was my dream. To wear a brown shirt and march. I said to myself, no, I am different. And this was why I was, but now I will make it up. So I did. I started my new book's introduction about Bialik, the leading Jewish Zionist poet. All over Israel there are streets with his name, not streets honoring Janusz Korczak because he went like a sheep guiding his people. For me, Korczak is a big hero, but for them, not. I don't know for whom to be more sorry—for the people that hid like rats and died like rats, or for the people that were killed in a pogrom. I was hidden like a rat and I would have been happy if my parents had been hidden like rats and not fought. I want to avoid death for them, for my parents, and my friends. How to live heroically, not how to die heroically. So I learned, and I admit to it, I also had a high hope for Zionism. But the doors of Palestine were closed for the survivors. The fact is that

someone writes that a thousand children could not be taken
in. My grandfather went to Palestine in 1930, came back
within a year, sick with malaria. He was one of the first
builders. They did not want every Jew from Germany or from
Austria or from Poland. And by the way, you can read, and it
is documented, that Egypt, Syria, a lot of countries wanted to
take in Jews. But we did not want it. We wanted to go to
America. And further, even if Jews wanted to come, how
many Jews could they take in Palestine even today, after forty
years of nationhood? A 100,000, 200,000, not millions. England made the mistake, said open the door. They wouldn't
have gotten the hundred thousand. But let us say they got
them. Even today the American government has had to pay
for 10,000 Fallasha (Ethiopian) Jews. That's forty years after
establishing a country with the three and a half million—
not in 1933, '35. But still today we lecture about how Palestine was closed. And last week a professor from the university called me up—Leon, is it true in Palestine they did
not allow. . . . And I said, "Listen, get off of your high horse.
How many Jews could Palestine have taken in? 50,000?
10,000?" I was in Israel last year and they told me, "We can
be killed in two ways. One way is not to have any immigra-
tion. You know, we need people. The other way is to take in
a million and a half Jews. We would have to say forget it
because we couldn't take in that many and now we would
have been killed the other way." They're making a mistake.
That's today, forty years after, and America is still putting in
money.

Can you imagine that they're happy? German Jews did not
want to go to Israel. The Polish Jews did not want to. Pioneers, yes, but how many pioneers do you get? A few people?
Young people? Not my father with my mother and seven
children. Surely not. But when I said this to the professor he
said, "You are right. But still, forget about it. It's much nicer
to say they did not let us in." They did not press America to
take us in. They did not want Trujillo to take the children.
Palestine was opening the doors. But how many could have
gone into Palestine? You don't talk about it. But some of

them would have been saying, some of them to Trujillo,
"What's a hundred thousand?" I said, "How many would
Palestine take? 50,000? 10,000? That isn't nothing!" I said,
"How about 100,000?" You walk away. You don't talk. A
hundred thousand against six million? It's nothing. A small
percent. But Palestine could have taken in 10,000. Better than
nothing! You see, your answer—it's too much an emotional
problem and Palestine became the focus of American Jews.

HJC   Then, as I understand it, from your book and other
sources, even the people who wanted to settle Palestine were
selective about which Jews they wanted to let in.

LW   Yes. They could not take in my mother with seven
children to come and build. They needed pioneers, not people
to eat. Not people on Social Security. They did not need
people, young people, that don't want to work or wanted to be
lawyers or doctors. They needed people to work the ground.
They needed street cleaners. They did not need more lawyers. They did not need more economists. They did not need
doctors. So they had to be selective. They were for building. If
you hire today people to build you a building, you don't say I
need people. You say I need builders. I don't need paper
shufflers. You would be selective if you built something, too.

HJC   You accuse the Zionists of being selective in another way also.

LW   Yes. It's easy to accuse anybody who does not agree
with your viewpoint of self-hate, of all kinds of different
reasons. But they *were* selective in many ways. They wanted
exactly what they needed. Including Hadassah, which was
selective regarding doctors. They didn't want too many because they might create competition against their own. They
said, "If we bring doctors in for one year instead of two years,
they may set up a competitive clinic in Tel Aviv. And this, we
don't want. So better we don't bring them in."

HJC   And this is while people were dying.

LW   People were in Germany wanting to get out. And the
doctors of America said, "Why don't you bring them in?
Forget about what happens in two years and next year." They
said, "Yes, but we have to think what happens to us." And

when I speak today in Israel about it, they say, "But didn't we build a country?" You know the end justifies the means. If the Catholics say it, it is anti-Semitism. If Cardinal O'Connor says it, everybody jumps. If the Lubavitch says it—oh, he's not so smart. He made a mistake.

WHITNEY HARRIS

Whitney Harris was one of the principal members of the U.S. prosecution staff at the Nuremberg trials. During his interrogation of the head of the Interior Intelligence Service in the Third Reich, Otto Ohlendorf, a major breakthrough in the Allied case against the Nazi war criminals occurred. Ohlendorf confessed that he was responsible for the murders of 90,000 people, and the prosecution was able to build from there. Harris was also able to obtain a confession from Rudolf Hoess, the commanding officer of Auschwitz, who admitted responsibility for two and a half million deaths.

Harris graduated magna cum laude from the University of Washington and received his law degree from the University of California. Before his military service he was admitted to practice before the U.S. Supreme Court. After his naval discharge in World War II, Harris taught at Southern Methodist University. He then filled several executive posts for Southwestern Bell in Dallas and later in St. Louis, where he was to make his home in 1963. He is the author of *Tyranny on Trial* (1954), a book about the Nuremberg experience, as well as *Family Law*.

He has earned numerous awards, including the Legion of Merit, the Officer's cross from the Federal Republic of Germany, and Poland's Medal of the War Crimes Commission. In

1954 he became the executive director of the American Bar Association, later a member of the International Bar Association, and came to serve on many boards, including the Japan-America Society of St. Louis, Phi Beta Kappa, and the St. Louis Holocaust Commission.

HJC "The privilege of opening the first trial in history for crimes against the peace of the world imposes a grave responsibility. The wrongs which we seek to condemn and punish have been so calculated, so malignant, and so devastating that civilization cannot tolerate their being ignored because it cannot survive their being repeated. That four great nations flush with victory and stung with injury stay their hands of vengeance and voluntarily submit their captive enemies to the judgment of the law is one of the most significant tributes that power has ever paid to reason." With these words Justice Robert Jackson opened the Nuremberg trials. Would you elaborate on what Justice Jackson meant by these words?

WH Undoubtedly, World War II was the greatest man-made catastrophe ever to occur. The leaders of the Allied Powers—the United States, Russia, and Great Britain—reached a decision during the course of the war that punishment would have to be imposed upon the perpetrators of the crimes of World War II. The initial decision was made at the Moscow Declaration on October 30, 1943. At that time it was agreed by Prime Minister Churchill, President Roosevelt, and Premier Stalin that those individuals who had committed crimes during the course of the war would be sent back to the countries in which their crimes were committed to be punished, and those whose crimes had no particular location would be punished by joint decision of the Allies. But no agreement was reached at that time whether this punishment would be in the form of executive action or whether the judicial process would be involved. Indeed, at this period the British were of the mind that executive action should be used. This was definitely the view of Prime Minister Churchill.

In the United States, however, the thought developed that a better record could be made of the crimes of the Nazi regime if the individuals who were responsible for the war and the crimes committed in the course of the war were brought to trial before an international tribunal. A memorandum was prepared as an aide memoir to President Roosevelt at the Yalta conference in January 1945. The judicial process was proposed as a means of determining guilt and arriving at punishment. Thus, the decision was reached in the United States that alleged war criminals should be brought to trial, and Justice Jackson, who had been appointed United States chief of counsel on May 8, 1945, firmly adhered to this view. He was able to persuade the British that this was the proper method of dealing with the Nazi war criminals. Consequently, at the conference which took place in the summer of 1945 leading to the organization of the international military tribunal, the position of the United States was that there should be a trial, and this position was accepted by the other powers. So when Justice Jackson says here that, "flushed with victory, we stayed the hand of vengeance," he meant that we would give these individuals who had committed tremendous crimes against humanity an opportunity to defend themselves, an opportunity they denied to others. That is the meaning of his opening remarks.

HJC At the Nuremberg trials there were twenty-two defendants.

WH There was a series of trials. We only dealt with twenty-two; twenty-four were indicted, twenty-two were brought to trial. It was never contemplated that there would be a series of international trials. That turned out to be the only international trial. The Allied Control Council for Germany enacted Control Council Law Number Ten, which gave authority to various occupation powers to conduct trials in their zones of occupation. Pursuant to Control Council Law Number Ten, the United States conducted a number of post-Nuremberg trials, as did the other Allied powers. These are what may be called the trial of secondary war criminals by occupation tribunals. These were not international trials.

The United States conducted fifteen such trials, with three American judges assigned to each trial.

HJC   There must have been quite a bit of resistance to the trials. Stalin himself suggested that the German staff be summarily executed. Joseph Pulitzer, the then-publisher of the *St. Louis Post-Dispatch*, suggested a round-up of a million, five hundred thousand Nazis and that they be executed. So there had to be pressure on the American officials.

WH   There was pressure. And, in the United States, Henry Morgenthau was a firm champion of executive action. Fortunately, for the cause of justice, this arbitrary method was not used. After all the evidence was in at the major trial, the tribunal acquitted three of the accused. The cause of justice would not have been served by using arbitrary action against persons suspected of being arch-criminals. The evidence might not have supported their convictions. At Nuremberg, three defendants were acquitted, seven were imprisoned, and only twelve received the death sentence.

HJC   Three types of crimes were defined: crimes against peace, war crimes, and crimes against humanity. How was that determined?

WH   Crimes against peace involved, essentially, the waging of aggressive war. That had an interesting aspect. Waging aggressive war constituted, in part, the violation of treaty agreements not to attack one's neighbor. Germany had such agreements with practically every nation that she attacked, and there was considerable discussion in London as to whether the crime of waging aggressive war should be included at all. It was sufficient, the French believed, that we could prove that the Germans attacked Poland in violation of the non-aggression treaty between Poland and Germany. And the French believed that to name aggressive war as a specific crime would be ex post facto. There was no law in existence at the time the charter was drafted which declared that waging aggressive war is an international crime. The French were very much concerned about this. Justice Jackson's position was that he would forgo the trial rather than to have the charge of aggressive war eliminated. He believed that it was absolutely essential at this period in history that the responsible powers should declare, once and for all, that waging aggressive war, whether or not in violation of a treaty, is an international crime. Ultimately, the French did give way on this point; and waging aggressive war was included as a separate crime in addition to violation of treaties and assurances in international law. This was a very significant advance in international law, and was due entirely to the strong position taken by Justice Jackson at that time.

War crimes are a different thing. We've had many treaties dealing with war crimes which involve primarily the mistreatment of soldiers. Crimes against humanity involve a somewhat different concept and are concerned primarily with the mistreatment of civilians during war. It is important to realize that the International Military tribunal did not deal with crimes against humanity, only when connected with one of the other crimes in the indictment—either waging aggressive war or committing war crimes. Consequently, in dealing with crimes against humanity, the tribunal did not go back into the prewar period.

HJC The Soviets were a little concerned about this, weren't they, because they wanted to be sure to protect themselves against charges of crimes against Finland and Poland.

WH Yes, that problem did arise in the negotiations in London and throughout the negotiations. General Nikitchenko, who was the chief Soviet delegate, took the position [that] the International Military Tribunal should only deal with war crimes committed by the Axis powers. He wanted the charter drafted to state that waging aggressive war is only a crime when committed by the Axis powers. Justice Jackson refused to accept this limitation and declared that he would not go forward with the trial if the Russians adhered to that position. Nonetheless they did not ever really back down, except at the last day of the negotiations, when it was finally agreed that the charge of aggressive war would be in general terms; that is, that anyone who waged aggressive war would be liable to be charged with a war crime, but that the jurisdiction of the International Military Tribunal would be restricted to such crimes when committed by the European Axis. Justice Jackson won his point that the decision of the Tribunal would have to declare aggressive war as a general crime. And General Nikitchenko protected the Soviets in the sense that the International Military Tribunal would never have jurisdiction over the aggressions the Soviets committed in Poland and Finland.

HJC How did you determine the type of evidence that would be either allowed or emphasized? I understand that, in general, documentary evidence—that is evidence taken from the German files themselves—would be given more weight than the evidence of eyewitnesses.

WH When we were preparing for this trial, obtaining evidence was the most critical matter. It's one thing to say that these people committed crimes. It's another thing to appear before a court of justice and prove that they committed crimes by evidence beyond a reasonable doubt—which was the test that was adopted at Nuremberg. We were successful in obtaining documentary evidence against the defendants. We were constantly finding incriminating documents. In fact, Justice Jackson became convinced that we were going to be able to prove the basic case through captured German documents. What better evidence could one have than that? The other idea of using live witnesses was not cast aside, but Justice Jackson decided that we would try to prove the basic case through captured German documents, supplemented with the testimony of witnesses. This gave rise to the withdrawal, by the way, of General Donovan as one of the principle aides of Justice Jackson shortly after the trial began.

HJC He preferred witnesses?

WH He preferred to proceed through witnesses and to conduct the trial more or less as we are accustomed to in the United States—putting witnesses on the stand and then introducing documents through the witnesses. What we did as lawyers was to prepare briefs containing documentary evidence—supporting the charges against the particular individual or organization. And that constituted the heart of the American case—and the heart of the entire case, in fact.

As a consequence, we have built a record which has stood for forty years and, in my opinion, will stand for four thousand more years.

HJC In your, I must say really excellent, book *Tyranny on Trial*, you mention that 485 tons of documents were located.

WH Yes. These documents were found all over Germany. I myself went out and dug up documents which had been buried. I went to Gestapo offices and searched through the refuse to find documents. Essentially, I was looking for execution orders signed by my defendant. But the greatest source of documents was from the United States Army, units of which discovered caches of documents.

HJC How was all of this done?

WH As they proceeded, they would go into different military establishments, and they would take all the files that they had, and bring them out, and then these files had to be analyzed. The documents had to be translated and organized. We had to assign file numbers to them. We had a large document room. The same documents were furnished to the defense. So it was a tremendous task on the part of the prosecution to assemble these documents and make them available to the Tribunal as evidence.

HJC Part of your task was to interview some of these worldwide criminals. One of the people you talked to and got a confession from was Rudolph Hoess, the commandant of Auschwitz.

WH His case was very interesting. It came late in the proceeding. In fact, after we had closed our case, and we then no longer had any right to introduce evidence, I learned that Rudolph Hoess had been captured by the British and I asked that he be sent to Nuremberg so that we might have the chance to interview him. I spent three days talking to him and ultimately reduced his testimony into the affidavit, which was subsequently introduced in evidence. A duplicate original of this affidavit is in my library at Washington University on the Third Reich. At this time Rudolph Hoess told me that two and a half million people had been killed at Auschwitz.

HJC Do you have any recollection of your impression of talking to maybe the greatest mass-killer of all time?

WH Yes, I think he was the greatest mass-killer of all time. There isn't any doubt of it. Rudolph Hoess had the appearance of a clerk. He was not an impressive individual at all, [not] in any sense. He wasn't aggressive, particularly. He had, of course, spent his lifetime, really, in the concentration camp business. That was his career. As a young man he had wanted to go into the military. He was a member of the Freikorps after World War I and was involved in the murder of an individual who supposedly had given information against the Freikorps. Starting in 1933 he became a member of the S.S. and went to Dachau. He was a concentration camp guard there at Dachau. Subsequently, he was sent to Saxenhausen in a higher position. Finally, he was sent, by Himmler, to Auschwitz before it was established as a murder camp.

And then in the summer of 1941, Rudolph Hoess told me, he was called to Berlin to see Heinrich Himmler, the head of the S.S. Hoess was in awe. He told me that Himmler told him that the Germans had a secondary war, in effect, against the Jews; that it was necessary that the Jews be eliminated; and that he was to return and establish at Auschwitz a center for the murder of Jews who would be sent there by train. Hoess said that he went to Treblinka to find out how this was accomplished at Treblinka. There he discovered that combustion engines were connected to rooms where the people were killed by carbon monoxide gas. He said that was a very inefficient way. When he got to Auschwitz, where huge rooms were built as killing centers, it was discovered that Zyklon B gas, which was an insecticide, when heated up, would quickly kill people, and that's what they used at Auschwitz.

HJC And what was his attitude while he was telling you these things? Was there great remorse?

WH No—I would not say that Rudolph Hoess showed remorse. He simply took the position, which was the general position of all subordinates to whom I talked during this period, that he was carrying out superior orders. When

Himmler said this had to be done, then that was his war-task and, no matter what, he had to carry it out.

HJC   That was a repeated defense to hide behind, and that was one of the things that the Nuremberg Trials judged against, isn't it? You could not hide behind the excuse that "I was ordered to do so."

WH   Absolutely. In fact, the charter of the International Military Tribunal declared that superior orders would not be a defense. Of course, acting in accordance with superior orders might be mitigating, but would not be a defense to any criminal act. And that's what the charter provided and that's what the Tribunal enforced.

HJC   Another precedent, at the Nuremberg Trial, was that heads of states were accountable for certain actions.

WH   Prior to this trial, it had been pretty much traditional that heads of state were considered to act for the state, not in their individual capacity. Therefore, whatever the state does may be wrong and you can take military action or apply sanctions against the state, but you are not supposed to do anything against the responsible individual who is acting for and in the name of the state. Nuremberg wiped that out completely and, from now on, a head of state may not claim that he's only acting for the nation. He is personally responsible.

HJC   Perhaps it might be appropriate to recognize some of the other precedents that the Nuremberg Trials set: It is a crime to initiate and wage aggressive warfare; it is a crime to be involved in a conspiracy to wage aggressive warfare, to violate the ordinary customs of war; and, of course, it is a crime to commit inhuman acts against civilians. Another important element is this: The Nuremberg Trials showed that a person charged with such crimes was entitled to a fair trial and not to summary execution. It is also interesting, I think, to note that the people of West Germany (as you point out in your book) accepted these findings and these decisions and, in fact, it has become part of the West German judicial tradition, as it were. Some people have thought that there might be the possibility of the charge that laws were framed

that would refer to prior crimes—ex-post-facto laws. How do
you escape that charge?

WH   The doctrine of ex-post-facto applies to municipal
law. It is applied in almost every country. You cannot bring
someone to trial unless what he has done was known to him
to be criminal at the time he does it. That's a simple element
of justice. Now we do not have, in international society, any
legislative body. Therefore, the doctrine of ex-post-facto has
no application in international law—except as an element of
justice. The most fundamental point here is that to adopt the
doctrine of ex-post-facto, to deny the possibility of punishing
these men guilty of these terrible crimes of World War II,
would have been, itself, an act of injustice.

We could not permit this doctrine, derived from municipal
law, to supersede what was the right course of action against
those persons who were responsible. That is the underlying
point. But there was a body of law extant at the time which
declared aggressive war to be criminal. The principle treaty
was the Kellogg-Briand pact of 1928. Germany was a signatory to that pact, which provided that the use of force in
international law would be outlawed. Each signatory to that
part agreed that military action would not be taken against
its neighbors. That law was in effect at the time Hitler committed his depredations and, consequently, the Tribunal
felt that the treaty, supported by several other international
agreements declaring war an international crime, was sufficient to overcome the argument that the proceeding was ex-
post-facto.

HJC   Western legal philosophy seems to include the no-
tion that for every legal wrong, there's a legal remedy. But the
remedy could not be adequate at Nuremberg.

WH   How can you expiate the murder and killing of
twenty-five million people and the devastation of an entire
continent? Twelve individuals were convicted of that crime
and received the death sentence at Nuremberg. Obviously,
there's no balance here. But the law did apply as best it might
have applied to those who were primarily responsible for
bringing about this episode in history, and justice was meted

out as best we were able to do it at the time. It must be remembered that not only did we have this major trial, and not only did we also have other trials by the occupying powers, but Germany itself underwent a massive program of "de-Nazification," and this proceeding was based upon the principles of law established at the Nuremberg Trial. All of those who participated as members of criminal organizations received varying forms of punishment in Germany. And, indeed, we find that forty years after the trial, there still is action being taken in Germany itself against those who may be found—even at this late date—to have had a participating role in the crimes of the Hitler regime.

HJC How do you feel about that? People say that somebody who is found now is in his eighties, is sickly—should that person be brought to trial?

WH To my mind, the passage of time has no hearing whatsoever upon the question of punishment. The only factor there is the ability of the person, perhaps, to defend himself. That's all. But to suggest that these individuals, like Mengele, who had succeeded in hiding out in South America for forty years, should not be brought to trial seems to me to be completely outrageous. Every individual who had a responsible role in the Nazi regime and can be found today and brought to trial should be made to answer for his crimes.

HJC Were the Nuremberg Trials, as history, more important, even, than they were as a trial? They set a precedent from the view of history of law that may even be more important than the outcome of the trials.

WH Yes, I think that you have a good point there. We are never going to have peace in this world unless law replaces force. And the great contribution of Nuremberg was that it did elevate law and justice above force and injustice. And we must have a rule of law in international affairs, or, as I have said, we're going to live forever in a world of force under a pall of fear.

HJC I'm reminded of the quote you have in your book from Justice Jackson, who says that the real complaining party at the bar is civilization.

WH   Civilization. Correct.

HJC   It's not just a matter of the Allies bringing this on, but even future generations want to be heard.

WH   That's absolutely right. And we must strive constantly to elevate law as the means of resolving disputes in international affairs so that the possibility of these terrible wars and all of the incidents related thereto—in this case, the Holocaust, one of the greatest tragedies of all time, maybe the greatest single tragedy of all time—can never occur again.

HJC   Have the Nuremberg Trials had an impact on the philosophy of law? Or do we have to wait until there's another world war and another similar trial to feel that impact?

WH   The Assembly of the United Nations has approved the principles of law enunciated by the charter of the International Military Tribunal and by the court in its decision. That is now the law of the United Nations itself. So we have the precedent firmly established. What we do not have, at this point, and what I have urged for many years, is an international court of criminal justice. We do not have that in being. One of the criticisms of the trial after World War II was that the court was an ad hoc tribunal of the victors. It doesn't seem fair to some that the winning country should set up its own tribunal, with its own judge, and try the people who have been defeated. I think this is a valid criticism, although trial by victors was unavoidable at the end of World War II. There was no court in existence at that time before which these persons could be brought to trial, and it was impossible to find impartial jurists anywhere. The whole world was involved in this war. But for the future it would be, in my view, highly desirable if we did have an international court of criminal jurisdiction in existence so that if there were conflicts that arose where a trial might be appropriate, we would have the judges already pre-selected.

HJC   What do you think the chances are for something like that occurring?

WH   Well, there's no chance at all at this time in history, but someday we will have it.

HJC The question of whether fair trials were possible at that time has been raised. The defendants—did they have an opinion about these trials?

WH It's fair to say that most of them realized that this was their only chance. If there had not been a trial, they probably would have been executed. So, from that standpoint, the defendants were satisfied that they had the trial and the opportunity to defend themselves. Some, like Goering, were pleased that there was a trial because it afforded him a basis to try to further his philosophy of Nazism, even at that time. So I don't think that it would be right to say that the defendants were opposed to the trial. On the contrary, I think they were happy that there was a trial. The only thing they were unhappy about was that they happened to be the defendants at the trial.

HJC Three of the twenty-two defendants at the Nuremberg Trials were acquitted. In your opinion, was that because they were innocent or because something in the trial allowed them to get off?

WH No, I think that probably the decision of the Tribunal was correct in the case of Schacht and von Papen. Schacht had withdrawn from the Nazi regime, really, before Hitler announced his firm declaration to wage aggressive war, and von Papen spent the war in Turkey as ambassador. He was also out of it. We could not prove that either Schacht or von Papen really had much to do with the regime during its criminal period. Schacht had a lot to do with advancing Hitler in the early years, but that wasn't criminal. Fritzsche was a special case. He had been captured by the Russians. He was one of only two that the Russians had: Raeder and Fritzsche. And it was desired to have some individual representing the propagandistic agencies of the Nazi regime as a defendant. Unfortunately, Goebbels, his wife, and their five children were all killed. The Russians said that they had Goebbels's right-hand man, Hans Fritzsche. We had never heard of Fritzsche, but nevertheless he was accepted as a defendant. It turned out that he was really nothing much more than a radio announcer in Berlin. So Fritzsche did not have a major role in the proceeding at all and was properly acquitted.

HJC   What personal impact did participating in the trials have on you at the time of the trials?

WH   Many of these events, these facts, were new to me. I spent the entire war in the Navy except toward the end, when I was assigned to the Office of Strategic Services. I knew nothing much about any crimes that were committed by the Nazis except the crime of aggressive war. We all knew that well enough. So these things really opened my eyes. I think that the greatest shock that I had in the whole proceeding was just before the trial opened when I interviewed Otto Ohlendorf.

My case dealt with the Gestapo and the SD and the over-all agency—the Reichssicherheitshauptamt, or the RSHA (Reich Main Security Office), the chief of which was Ernst Kaltenbrunner. And this office was divided into various sub-offices, and one of those, Amt VI, was headed by a man by the name of Ohlendorf, according to a document which I had found. I learned that Ohlendorf had been taken captive by the British and was being interrogated in Britain by British Intelligence. I asked that Ohlendorf be sent to Nuremberg so that I might have a chance to talk to him, to find out more about this organization. They did send Ohlendorf to Nuremberg, and I did interrogate him. I had learned by this time from a document sent by a man by the name of Becker back to the RSHA complaining about how a gas van had failed to function, that there were gas vans used by the SD and the Gestapo in the eastern territories—to kill people. This came from an Einsatz group commander. Ohlendorf was the first person that I interrogated at length at Nuremberg, and I simply started out by asking his life history, and he told me what he had done. He joined the SS, and then he had become head of the SD when he was thirty-seven, and he continued in this position except for one year, 1941. I asked him what he did in that year, and he said he was the commandant of Einsatzgruppen D that year. I knew enough then to ask him this simple question: "How many men, women and children did you kill that year?" And he answered, "90,000." And that broke the whole case as far as Einsatzgruppen and everything else. From that time on Ohlendorf was my witness, and we had all the evidence right then. That was the greatest shock that I had at Nuremberg. Everything else was incidental to that confession.

HJC Why did he confess?

WH I don't know why he confessed. Why did Rudolph Hoess tell me that he killed two and a half million people? He didn't have to say that. As far as I could see, there seemed to be a willingness on the part of most of the Germans to admit the facts and to try to defend themselves on the basis that they couldn't avoid doing what they did because this was their war-duty, and they were required to do this as part of their war-duty. That was always the excuse of every defendant.

HJC Some years later Eichmann was captured by the Israelis and brought to trial. How did you feel about that trial?

WH I was delighted that they captured Eichmann and brought him to trial. Eichmann was a very significant figure in our proceeding because it was Eichmann who was in charge of rounding up, primarily, the Jews of Europe to send them to extermination centers—mainly to Auschwitz. So Eichmann was a top war criminal. Not only that, but it was Eichmann's testimony which gave us the figure of six million persons who had been killed by the Germans. Even Rudolph Hoess, the commandant of Auschwitz, relied upon Eichmann for the number of people who had been killed at Auschwitz. Eichmann's position was that there were four million killed at the camps and two million had been killed in the fields. Perhaps the figures are too high. It doesn't matter. The number killed was astronomical. But Eichmann was a very significant individual, properly apprehended; properly, in my view, spirited away from Argentina and brought to trial. And I'm pleased that he was tried and convicted and executed.

HJC His defense was that he was just following orders.

WH His defense was the same as all of them—that he only followed orders, that's all. That he had nothing to do with killing. Eichmann's defense was that his job was simply to go into the various towns, get the people, put them on trains, and then that was the end of it. Where the trains went, he said, didn't concern him.

HJC You have a unique perspective on all of the evidence, the tons, the hundreds of tons of evidence, talking to the defendants, hearing the confessions. Between that time and now, you have seen a growing body of literature—not significant, but nevertheless there—that says that there are doubts about whether any of this ever took place. How do you respond to all that?

WH This is so false that there's no basis to it. No one is going to believe it. There's no one in Germany who would believe this nonsense. We all know what happened. The facts are there, the evidence is there. The transcript of the Nuremberg proceeding consists of forty-five volumes. That's the transcript. In addition, we have other volumes with the documents alone. These transcripts have been translated into German. They are in Germany and they have all been bought. I haven't been able to get one recently. The evidence can never be controverted. People can quarrel, maybe, over how many people were killed here and how many people were killed there—that's trivial, doesn't amount to anything. The basic outline is clear. This was the worst case of aggression that you could find, when Hitler attacked Poland. It was so clear, there's no doubt about it. Germany was incontrovertibly guilty of waging aggressive war under Hitler. And the crimes that were committed against the Jews and other people by the Hitler regime have been supported by so much evidence, they can never be controverted.

HJC One of the interesting facts about what happened at Nuremberg is that the power of the victors was not abused. There was not the summary execution that Stalin wanted, that Morgenthau wanted, even Joseph Pulitzer wanted. To what do you attribute that?

WH I attribute this to the legal profession to which I'm very happy to say I belong. These men who served as judges at Nuremberg and, indeed, the men who served as prosecutors, all put the law first. No one tried to do anything other than to produce the true evidence. There was no purpose of vindictiveness on the part of anyone. Now it may be said that the conviction of these top men, such as Goering, was inevitable, but if it was inevitable it was because of the evidence. That is all. Not because of any pre-position that any of these men had taken. And indeed, I want to make clear that the Tribunal insisted throughout that everything that we advocated be proved by evidence. The judgment of the Tribunal itself recites the basic evidence upon which the Tribunal arrived at its decision. So I think that we can rest in confidence that the integrity of the legal profession is what made the Nuremberg Trial the great precedent that it is today.

HJC For the record, who were the defense attorneys?

WH The defense attorneys were all German lawyers. Each defendant had a right to select his own defense attorney and they could be members of the Nazi party.

HJC What was your opinion about how they conducted themselves?

WH For the most part they conducted themselves in an exemplary manner. Some of them were brilliant, such as Jahreis, who conducted most of the legal discussions. He was an outstanding lawyer. There were one or two we thought were not effectual. But, essentially, they presented their cases in an honorable manner and they insisted on the proof of evidence. When an issue became hotly controverted, such as the Katyn Forest massacre, they fought very hard for their principles and they did very well for their clients.

HJC How did you communicate? There must have been some language barriers there.

WH Well the whole proceeding was conducted through the mechanics of instantaneous translation. This was the first time that it had ever been used in any international proceeding. This was done through banks of translators, who instantaneously translated the testimony of every witness into the various languages used in the proceeding. All participants had headphones and a dial so that they could dial to the language that they wanted to hear. If we were interrogating a German witness, and we were speaking in English, we would have ours on English and he would have his on German, and so forth. In this way, everyone was able to understand everyone else instantaneously. We had to have lights on the lawyer's podium and on the judge's bench warning us—a yellow light, if we were going too fast, and finally, if the translation broke down, a red light would flash and we would stop. In this way the trial proceeded in several languages.

HJC   What was the feeling—I mean, you came in touch with, of course, Americans whom you didn't know, but also British and French and Soviets—what was the feeling among the prosecutors there and the judges?

WH   I think that in general everyone got along quite well. There was some camaraderie, but not a reat deal because most of us were working so hard that we were concentrating on our own business. We each had our own segments. The United States had the responsibility of proving the central plan, the general conspiracy, the common plan. And this embraced the entire case, really. The British had the responsibility of proving aggressive war in violation of treaties, and the French had war crimes and crimes against humanity in the West, and the Soviets had war crimes and crimes against humanity in the East. We all did our work pretty much separately, in our own teams. But we did get to meet the members of the other prosecution staffs.

HJC   Have you kept in touch with any of the colleagues?

WH   Yes, I have, over the years. But you understand that most of those who were with us at Nuremberg are now dead. All the chief prosecutors, except Sir Hartley Shawcross, are dead. And there are not too many trial counsel who are still alive—only the young ones, like I was.

HJC   I asked earlier what it had meant to you to be a part of the trials. What has it meant to you now from this perspective?

WH   Justice Jackson, in the introduction to my book, said that he felt that the years—and here was a Chief Justice of the Supreme Court of the United States speaking—that the years that he spent at Nuremberg were the most meaningful and constructive of all of the years of his life. I think that all of us who had that experience probably would place those years—some were not there the whole time, I was—as the most significant period of our professional careers. These were momentous events that simply stagger the imagination. And it was dramatic. Also, I think that we accomplished a great good for humanity. The poem goes that: "Truth, crushed to earth, shall rise again / The eternal years of God are hers / But Error, wounded, writhes in pain, / And dies among his worshippers" [William Cullen Bryant, "The Battlefield"]. Hitler, and those who associated with him, are dead. That era has gone, I hope forever. What we did at Nuremberg in exposing Hitler and the crimes of his colleagues and his associates is certain to advance the cause of truth and justice in the world.

HJC Thank you for that eloquent explanation and thank you for what you did for all of us.

LEO EITINGER

Dr. Leo Eitinger was born in Czechoslovakia in 1912. In 1939, at the age of twenty-seven, he fled his native country for Scandinavia to escape the Nazi threat. He was captured in Norway and spent much of the war in Auschwitz, where he was able to survive by exchanging identities with a dead, non-Jewish victim. He is one of the world's greatest authorities on the psychological impact of the Holocaust experience on survivors.

After initially studying philosophy, Eitinger earned a degree in medicine at the Masaryk University in Brno, Czechoslovakia. After World War II he specialized in psychiatry and earned an M.D. from the University of Oslo in 1958. He worked in several hospitals and became a professor of psychiatry and superintendent of the department of the Medical School in Oslo, 1949 to 1984. Eitinger is the recipient of many honors including the King's Gold Medal, the Brno University honorary medal, the Bergen-Belsen International Award, the Hebrew University of Jerusalem Remembrance Medal, and the Commander of Order of the Royal Norwegian St. Olav, 1978. He was made an honorary member of the Australia and New Zealand Association for Forensic Psychiatry and has served as president of both the Norwegian Psychiatric Association and the Nordic Psychiatric Congress. His writings, available in English, include *Studies in Neuroses* (1955), *Concentration Camp Survivors in Norway and Israel* (1964), and *Mortality and Morbidity after Excessive Stress* (1973), as well as many authoritative monographs.

HJC   You were a medical doctor when you were taken prisoner?

LE   Yes, I took my medical degree in 1937 in Czechoslovakia. Then I began my military service, which was interrupted by the occupation of the Germans. I fled to Norway. In Czechoslovakia I used to work with a group of people who helped German refugees who escaped to Czechoslovakia and who then via Norway, helped by the so-called "Nansen-Aid," continued their migration from Norway to overseas.

HJC   Were these mainly Jewish people?

LE   No. There were both Jews and non-Jews, active politicians, Social Democrats, people who were working for human rights. There were very few Jews in Norway. Then suddenly we were refugees ourselves and we were admitted to Norway. I got a Norwegian visa in a rather complicated way having to do with my being a medical doctor. I couldn't get exit permission from the Nazis for a long time. I arrived in Norway in November 1939. I started to learn Norwegian and work in a hospital. Then Norway was invaded in April 1940, and I was on the run again. I tried to hide out, but finally I was caught, arrested, and went through different prisons and concentration camps in Norway before I was deported to Auschwitz.

HJC   Do you recall the incident of your treating the young Elie Wiesel at Auschwitz?

LE   Yes. Of course, I didn't know that it was Elie when I met him. I heard it the first time when you and I and the others were together at the meeting in Long Island ["A Conference on the Work of Elie Wiesel and the Holocaust Universe," September 7-9, 1976].

HJC   That's the first time he told you, yet he knew all that time?

LE   Yes. He recognized me in Oslo.

HJC   How did you meet in Oslo?

LE   He was invited to give a lecture. He was standing there very modestly, and then he got up and started to speak—you know, when Elie starts to speak he changes completely. You have the feeling that he doesn't speak himself; it speaks through him. He talked about Buchenwald.

I had some relatives who were in London during the war. One of them was a member of the Czech government. I hoped that I could come from Buchenwald to London through his help. So I went to Rabbi Schechter [the chaplain] and said: "These children are in real danger—not a danger to life now but a danger to be demoralized and we must do something, must try to bring them into some organized way of life." So he wrote a letter of recommendation to the Zionist organization in England asking them to take care of these children in Buchenwald. One of these children was Elie but that I *didn't* know.

I did not go to England because my own letter to my relative in London did not arrive. So I returned to Norway, where I had been arrested. In Buchenwald there had been Norwegian non-Jewish prisoners. They were liberated at the beginning of March 1945 by the Swedish Red Cross. But we were a group of five Norwegian Jews and we were not liberated but stayed there until the liberation by the American army.

When Elie gave his lecture in Oslo, I talked to him afterwards and told him that we had been in Buchenwald at the same time and that I had Schechter's letter. I asked Elie if he would like to see it. So we met the next day, but he didn't mention anything about Auschwitz. I knew that he came from Auschwitz, on the same transport, but until the 1976 meeting on Long Island I didn't know the full story.

I remembered it very well because he was such a sweet young boy, helpless and completely different from all the others—not of the pushing type, but you really felt that he was a nice boy. I was sitting at his bedside and telling him stories. He wanted to know if he would survive his operation or not. I never lie to a patient. I said, "Look at me, I'm telling you the truth." And what is written there is really verbatim. I went with him to the operation because he was such a child.

HJC Did you perform the operation?

LE No. But I was standing there and helping.

HJC Without anesthetic!

LE Yes. Holding hands was sort of anesthetic. Then the transport came, everything was in disarray, and, of course, I lost track of him.

HJC Had you heard of him before that talk?

LE I had heard his name but it didn't make a deep impression. I must confess that after the war I read several books of survivors and what I read was more or less, let's say, egocentric, full of self-pity. So in the beginning I actually tried to avoid reading about things. I had to work it through. I myself sat down in the summer of 1945 and wrote my own story—just in order to get rid of it and have it finished.

As a psychiatrist, of course, I was concerned with the question which we have discussed many times with others: How could one live again after the war?

I made various investigations and wrote books about these problems. Then, about ten years after my liberation, I felt strong enough to approach the real problem of influence of the camps on human beings. From that time on, I could not stop working with this problem.

HJC When you went back to the literature you found *Night*. That must have made a great impact on you because it wasn't like other books that you had read.

Are you surprised to know that *Night*, when it was first published, in Argentina, in Yiddish, was 800 pages long?

LE No.

HJC You were talking about the oversentimentalizing of earlier writers. Maybe it was, when he first published it—I don't know. In the English edition, the memoir is 109 pages.

LE Every word is really as strong as a word can be.

HJC Perhaps when *Night* was 800 pages long, every word was not as strong as it could be.

LE I really don't know. A person with his sensitivity and his faculty of observation could write thousands of pages and still always say something new, really new, humanly new.

HJC You mentioned Wiesel's helping of his father in the death camp. I asked him how guilty he felt about his first reaction when his father died, that instant of relief—obviously a very natural kind of thing. But he does mention it in *Night,* and I think he is working it out in several of his novels. He disagreed. But in his latest novel, *The Testament,* it seems to me to be all right there. I even wondered whether the "death" of God and the death of Elie's father occurred at the same time for him.

LE   Yesterday I discussed with Elie and with Robert Jay Lifton [psychiatrist] how extremely difficult it was to remain a human being. I don't blame those who didn't—that would be preposterous. People like doctors, nurses, and so on, who had the possibility to care for others, to keep their original values even in this madhouse, were the fortunate ones. But those people who, in one way or another, were able to stick to their original values, in spite of everything, perhaps with small deviations (which were necessary) and feeling as Elie describes immediately after the death of his father, these are the people, I think, who have less neurotic disturbances after the war than the others.

HJC   We read studies of people who lost their values in the camps and of those who gained values in the camps.

LE   This is actually one of the problems which I don't completely understand. I know that it happened. But, let's say from a purely scientific point of view, from a purely psychiatric or psychological point of view, I don't understand it.

HJC   And you have studied it for several decades.

LE   I have discussed the question with probably hundreds of Norwegian survivors. They don't call themselves survivors; they call themselves ex-prisoners, because the mortality rate was relatively low for the non-Jewish Norwegians. The really positive aspect is, for them, to have proven comradeship, friendship. But this was more difficult or nearly impossible, under the most extreme situations. This is actually for me such an enigma, nevertheless, to be able to grow in a human way.

HJC   Do you approach it in your writings?

LE   No.

HJC   The same thing happened with Livia Rothkirchen at Yad Vashem as happened with you. I was there doing research on atrocity photography for my book *A Christian Response to the Holocaust* and saw a photo that covers a large wall, of seventeen men lying in their bunks at liberation time. I think you've probably seen this picture. Weisel and Dr. Rothkirchen passed it by many times, over a several-year period, before he told her he was in that photograph. I asked Elie if I could write something about it and he said, "No." I wrote something and showed it to him and he gave me permission to publish it.

LE   I didn't know Elie is in the photo. I know that picture and I know who took it.

HJC   You know who took it?

LE   Yes. The photographer was Sivert Stockland. We were in Buchenwald after liberation. We once heard over the loud-speaker: "Are there any Norwegians in the camp? Please come to the main gate." So we went, these five Norwegian boys and I, and there was an American soldier, Sivert Stock-land, who told us that his parents were from Norway, his father was no longer alive, but his mother doesn't read or write English, only Norwegian. He wanted to write a letter and he didn't know Norwegian. So he wanted to find some Norwegians who could write a letter to his mother. And he took the pictures!

HJC   Is your wife a survivor?

LE   No, she was in London during the war. We knew each other from before the war. She was also from Czecho-slovakia. I actually died officially in Buchenwald. I have my death certificate. I changed my identity during the last days of Buchenwald. They tried to transport all of the Jews so as to evacuate the camp. So I took the identity of another Czech prisoner who had died—it was possible to do so in the last days. So my wife-to-be was in England and after the war she looked up the registers and saw that I was dead. Then she came to Sweden, to visit a sister there, and by chance, really by chance, she heard I was alive. After the war I wrote to the Red Cross and they sent me my death certificate.

HJC   How did you feel about seeing that?

LE   Well, you see I consider every day in my life as a gift, every single day, not deserved, just a gift.

HJC   I have been in Elie's apartment several times when people have called, once even from Paris, to tell him that a survivor had committed suicide. Do you find that happening very much? You talk about every day as a gift; I try to think about what would cause these people to despair. Is it something that they think they failed to do with this gift? Is it because the world has not gotten better, has learned nothing from the World War II experience?

LE   I think the disappointment of the survivors is immense. Elie has written about it. What he didn't mention is perhaps this extreme idealization of the world outside the camp; because he was so young he didn't realize this. But people who were in the camp several years idealized the world outside the camp in a completely uncritical way. You divided the world into inside the barbed wire and outside the barbed wire. Our expectations for the time to come—if there would be a future—were completely unrealistic. There would be only good in the world, they thought. Nothing bad could happen any more once the world realized what was happening here; everyone then must become a good person. They didn't express it in these words, of course, but this was actually the basic thought with which we were living.

Well, after this nothing bad could happen any more. On the one side because it is so bad that nothing worse can happen; on the other side because people must finally have learned that there is no other way than to be a decent person.

HJC   Why didn't more survivors commit suicide?

LE   Because life and the life instinct are very strong human forces and, as long as somebody is not completely isolated and has some connections with other people, somebody to live for, even if he is not living completely for the other but has some inter-human connections, suicide is rather difficult to commit.

DOROTHEE SOELLE

Dorothee Soelle, a leading German Protestant theologian, co-founded with her husband, Fullbert Stefensky, an ecumenical group called Political Evening Prayer, a movement of theological-political reflection and action. Her writings and lectures have made her a major figure in Jewish-Christian relations.

Ms. Soelle attended the University of Cologne and the University of Freiburg and earned a degree in philosophy in 1954 at the University of Goettingen. She taught and lectured in a number of German institutions and for many years split her time teaching between Germany and the United States, particularly at New York's Union Theological Seminary. Some of her many books are: *Christ the Representative* (1967), *The Truth is Concrete* (1969), *Beyond Mere Obedience* (1970), *Political Theology* (1974), *Suffering* (1975), *Choosing Life* (1982), *Of War and Love* (1983), *Thinking about God* (1990), and *The Window of Vulnerability* (1990). Professor Soelle held memberships in PEN and the Royal Scientific Academy of Utrecht and has been the recipient of many awards including a grant from the German Society for Research, the Theodore Heuss Medal, the Droste award for Poetry, Mursburg, and an honorary doctorate from the Protestant Faculty, Paris.

HJC   What is the impact that the Holocaust has on European Christian theology? Clearly, it has not made much of an impact in this country. What is the situation in Germany particularly and in Europe in general?

DS   I think it could have had more of an impact than it really has. In February 1982 the chairman of the Council of Protestant Churches in Germany, Bishop Lohse, gave a talk at Union Seminary about the question: "The Jewish Christ and the Christian Messiah." It was about the interrelatedness of the Christian and Jewish faiths. It made me completely speechless, because he managed to talk fifty minutes or so without even mentioning the Holocaust. *On this question.* And he gave his talk in a very academic, calm manner, trying to analyze the subject without any awareness of history. Afterwards, I went to him and asked him whether or not he could have given the same talk forty years ago in the same way. And he proudly replied, "Yes, it would be the same." And then I stopped asking, because I think that was just the utmost expression of not being attached at all to what is reality, to what I think is the major event in German history. I told him that I thought it was impossible to talk as a German and as a Christian about Jewish-Christian relationships without even mentioning one of the six million. But that's the reality of the official church: They dealt with that as a so-called "theological problem." I think in itself it is not bad will. It is a complete forgetfulness; of course it is a "repression," in Freudian terms. You don't want to remember. But also it's almost a theological technique to shelter yourself from reality.

HJC   This is going on with other issues as well.

DS   It surely does (right). I think that a lot of the political questions we're dealing with right now are related to this whole living without one's past. I mean, all these people a little older than myself came out of the war with this "never again" feeling. "Never again war, never again fascism!" That was the slogan we had in the late forties. And now, we in the peace movement are trying to dig that out again, but so many

people in the middle generation—ranging from say twenty-
five to fifty or so—have forgotten the "never again."

HJC   Do you find this true in other parts of Europe as
well?

DS   That's a complex question. I think it's surely not true
in those countries which were occupied and severely dam-
aged by the German invasion. Usually you remember the
things they did to you and not the things that you did to
them. That's one of the selective ways our memory func-
tions. So in Holland there's surely more awareness of what
war means, and there's surely also still some anti-German
feeling. I guess in France it is true in a similar way.

HJC   Paris has an archbishop who is born of a Jewish
family. Has that had any impact on this question as far as you
know? I'll tell you what Elie Wiesel told me about their
initial meaning. They had agreed not to publish anything
about the meeting. It lasted for about four hours but Elie said
that he began by asking the question: "Tell me, Archbishop,
are you our messenger to them or their messenger to us."

DS   Good question!

HJC   What about the impact of the Holocaust on European Jews? Surely they are not forgetting, using the analogy
that you used: those who receive the pain remember it more
than those who give it.

DS   That's a hard question for me to respond to because
the German-Jewish population is so small now that I'm not
too much in contact with them. There are a few around but
most, naturally, preferred to stay in the other countries. I
have certain very strong ties to Israel and know a lot of
European German Jews who went to Israel. For them there's
no way to forget this at any time. I remember when I first
went to Israel, in the fifties, I was with one of the first
German groups which was able to go there. I was with a
Jewish-Christian friendship group or something like that. We
went there and I was on the street in Jerusalem and lost my
way. I saw a woman coming toward me, and she looked so
European to me, and I spoke to her in German. Immediately

she turned around and left me standing there. She made it clear to me that she wouldn't talk to me. That was the first time that I was aware of what this whole thing of collective guilt or collective shame really means. I never felt so German and so bound to my nation. It's my father's tongue and my language, my homeland, fatherland—it is my history as well.

HJC   Do you see anything like a Jewish-Christian dialogue taking place in Europe? There is some of that in this country.

DS   There is some of that. I think during the first ten years after the Holocaust, between '45 and, say, up into the sixties, there was a serious effort on both sides—from the Christian side mainly—to work through and think through the history of anti-Judaism into anti-Semitism, and how this is rooted in the New Testament, specifically, and in some of Paul's writing. How far could we repeat the same things?

There was a very interesting move from the synod of the church in the Rhineland. They worked for an extended period of time on this Jewish-Christian question and finally ended up with a statement which clearly says that they don't want to do missionary work among Jews; that they would consider this as theologically wrong and why. And this was a very good move forward to clarify the issue. But then the faculty in Bonn, the Protestant faculty, made a countermove. They wrote a paper which was signed by the majority of this faculty talking in very high Christological terms—Christ alone, Christ the highest being, etc., etc.—and then taking an orthodox perspective. It was all very theological but, if you look through, I think it was very clear that they learned nothing out of the Holocaust. Nothing. It didn't change their theology. I think it's a good way to evaluate (at least in Germany) a person's theology if you ask the question whether or not he or she has changed anything in his or her theologizing through the Holocaust. And that includes some Christological questions: How would you perceive Christ? What would be Christ's relation to Jews? And it has also some theological sense in which questions like: "How would you see God, the almighty, powerful, supernatural being who is in heaven and could have stopped Auschwitz if he wanted to do so, and didn't do it—can you still deal with this God, *if that is God?*" I mean I don't think it is God, but some do. That's what I mean. How do these events change your own thought and concept of God? That's the deepest question of all of them.

HJC Jews themselves ask where God was at Auschwitz. In the camps we learn that God was put on trial. Some found him guilty of breaking the Covenant, others said this was the coming of the Messiah. It's very difficult.

DS Yes, it is. It is very difficult. Some of the most moving documents, including prayers, came down to us from the camps where some of them prayed even for their torturers. But it seems to me that there was a certain shift from an omnipotent—as I can see this very male—God towards the co-sufferer, a being who was not able to change this but is depending on us. And lives in it with us.

HJC Some of the things you said remind me of an experience I had here. Wen I was appointed by President Carter to the United States Holocaust Memorial Council, there was an article about that in the paper. And one of the quotations I gave to a reporter was that Jews asked where was God at Auschwitz. And I asked where was Christ at Auschwitz. And that was the headline of the article: "Where was Christ at Auschwitz?" And that got quite a response, as you can imagine. I got the usual hate letters, you know, wishing all my children had multiple sclerosis and things like that. But some of the letters that came in, of course, were very sincere. I remember one in particular from a seminarian who was concerned with the state of my soul, and wrote a very long detailed involved letter saying: "You know where Jesus was, he was hanging on a cross with the victims." And when I wrote to him I said that's not much consolation to Jews. But I responded more to a sentence he had in that letter, which I find in many of these sincere letters, the ones that are signed. Somewhere along the line there seems to be that code sentence: "They didn't accept Jesus, you know." And so I write back and say: "You're absolutely right, let's kill them all." And I get no correspondence back. It ends the discussion. But there is that feeling that they did not accept Jesus so they have to suffer.

DS It's the worst of Christian theology still to think in these terms. There's an undercurrent in the link between anti-Judaism in the New Testament (when Jews are identified as those who didn't accept Jesus) and modern anti-Semitism. I think that's not very easy to do for a historian—to bridge that—but it is necessary. Why was this new anti-Semitism coming in a special phase of industrialization, at least in industrialized countries like in Germany and Austria, where Hitler came from? What are the rules there and how is this related to Catholicism? I remember when I was about seventeen, in the cathedral at Cologne they played the St. Matthew Passion for the first time after the war. They omitted a chorus which says, "His blood may come on us and our children." It is a very powerful section in Bach's music but they just skipped it and I thought that was the right thing to do.

HJC Was there much of a reaction to that?

DS Yes, people asked and they got the response. At least the conductor of this performance knew what he was doing.

HJC It seems to be a much more complicated issue at the Oberammergau Passion Play. It would be so simple, it seems to me, to eliminate offensive passages and yet they find a number of reasons for not doing so.

DS I think in the specific situation I mentioned they couldn't do it. At this time my family had many Jewish friends so I was in contact with Jewish people, not so much before it all happened because I was too small then. But I grew up with a family with a lot of understanding. I had a pretty liberal kind of education and so almost everything was discussed in our house, between children and parents.

We were five and one time we had a birthday party. My mother insisted that we would invite two or three certain children. We children all agreed that they were stupid and we didn't like them. My mother said a very surprising thing: There would be no discussion about this. We never had this kind of demand and it took me five years before I learned that they were half Jews (as it was called). Later she said, "No one else will invite them, so you invite them." That was my meeting with Jews and being made aware of Jewish problems and what happens to Jews. This was one of the things I experienced through my parents. And so it led me into a deeper research later after it all, to find out the reasons. I really wanted also *to know.* That's an important point. I am getting so impatient when I meet people who don't know what "selection" or Zyklon B is. As Germans I hate them; I mean, they have to know that. They have to have some information about how it happened, how it was, when, with whom, etc., etc. To know the details. I mean I may be more impatient with people of my own generation than with very young people. But still I think they have to know some of the basic things. It's just a *must* for anyone who has a sort of conscience.

HJC   What must Christians do now to become reconciled with Jews?

DS   Well, I'll say never again Fascism and never again war. That's the most we can do. I mean, besides the things we did: reparations and the like on the legal level. There are still some questions about that. It could have been maybe more generous. There are all these borderline cases where people find out what they have now, and blame it on their exile, or the things they went through during the Nazi period. And they have these lawyers. I met a man in New York who had to do with that and he said it was terrible, because whether or not someone is entitled to get reparation or not and to—it's horrible. Like you put suffering, or hurt, or humiliations on a sort of scale to find out how much this is worth. I tell you, it's a strange business. But I think as a whole West Germany, for example, as compared to East Germany, did pretty well.

HJC   Parenthetically, let me say, I have a son who was injured at work. And he went to a union hall where they have a chart and each part of the body is listed as worth so much money.

DS   Yes, yes. But I think as a whole this strong feeling "never again"—. And yet the mentality of building up an

image of an enemy and using Jews as scapegoats has not died
out in my country. And how many people consider communists as the new Jews? What's wrong with killing communists? Nothing, eh? So there are some links between those
who resisted Hitler in the Confessing Church and others
who are working for peace.

HJC   Once you establish a principle of killing . . .

DS   Also, when you establish a principle of seeing some
other human beings as non-human beings, as rats or something, you can just go ahead and kill them. I think anti-
Communism is not only the greatest stupidity of the
twentieth century, as Thomas Mann said when he was in this
country, it's also a Fascist attitude.

HJC   Why do you find it the greatest stupidity?

DS   That's just a phrase of this great writer. But I think
it is an enormous blindness about what other people have
chosen in terms of their economy and their wish [of] how to
live. Even if you have severe criticisms against so-called
Communist countries—*as I do*—you still are not right in
this absolutely blind hate against Communism. You see this
in any move towards more peace and justice. If any of this
peace movement is seen as Communist . . .

I had a long talk with a conservative on the radio and the
only argument this man had against us in the peace-camp
was that we worked together with Communists. So I said,
"Listen, if a Communist doesn't like so much Napalm on the
skin of a baby and I happen not so much to like that as well,
why shouldn't we cooperate on this specific question? That
doesn't mean that I adopt all of his values, and all of his
convictions and doings and practices. But it means that we
cooperate on this specific thing." And I have to do that, and I
think it's really stupid not to build up alliances. Christians
and Jews and Communists were together in the concentration camps, after all. Reaganites were not. They were on the
other side.

EMIL FACKENHEIM

Dr. Emil Fackenheim was born in Halle, Germany, and has long been considered one of the premier Jewish theologians of the post–World War II period. His writings about the impact of the Holocaust on Jewish religious thinking have been widely influential.

Fackenheim attended the University of Halle (1937-1938), was ordained a rabbi in Germany the following year, and studied at the University of Aberdeen (1939-1940). Five years later he gained a Ph.D. from the University of Toronto, where he taught in the philosophy department for over thirty years. He and his wife, Rose, emigrated to Israel, where he continues a teaching and writing career. A former Guggenheim Fellow and member of the Royal Society of Canada, Dr. Fackenheim was also awarded the President's Medal of the University of Western Ontario for the best scholarly article published in Canada in 1954.

Among his books are: *Metaphysics and Historicity* (1961), *Quest for Past and Future* (1968), *The Religious Dimension of Hegel's Thought* (1968), *Encounters between Judaism and Modern Philosophy* (1973), *The Jewish Return into History* (1978), and *God's Presence in History* (1980). A sampling of Fackenheim's work, compiled by Michael L. Morgan, appears in *The Jewish Thought of Emil Fackenheim* (1987). He has published in numerous academic journals in the United States, Canada, Germany, and Israel.

HJC   Why should the Holocaust be regarded as a unique experience for Jews?

EF   For it to be unique in the framework of Jewish existence is one thing, but I think it's also unique without that framework. Therefore, if I put on my other hat, the philosopher's hat, I have to deal with this, too. But first a couple of basic philosophical preliminaries—one is almost tired repeating it, but it has to be done at the beginning. Every event is unique. Anybody will tell you this who does a couple of years in philosophy. Therefore, I used to tell my students: "If I were to try to describe in every detail, without omitting anything, what happened in the last five minutes, it would take me an infinity of time to do it." Therefore, you have to omit things. Not only that, the very use of words implies that the unique is unintelligible. When I say "this chair" it goes back to Aristotle, to try to understand what is substance. Aristotle has to say that this chair is just this chair and not any other chair. And yet, if he tries to define it or understand it, he has to pounce on the characteristics that are common with every other chair, or perhaps every other specimen of this category of chair. He can go to lowest species and then beyond *that*, he can just point. (Since people don't philosophize about the Holocaust, I have these preliminaries.)

To go on: there are what philosophers call "egocentric particulars." Namely, when I use the word "I," I don't mean anybody in general, any "I," I mean just me. When you use the same word "I," you mean yourself. These are well known things discussed in philosophy. Therefore when we come now, let's say from a discipline like mathematics or, for that matter, physics, or any discipline in sociology that deals with general patterns, to *history*, which is supposed to deal with particulars, any philosopher of history will tell you that you can describe but you can't define. When you write about the French Revolution, you don't write about revolutions in general, and you have quite a problem. This is one of the reasons

why some philosophers say history is really not a proper
science at all. Aristotle said that. For him it's lower than even
poetry because it deals with particulars. And the particular,
in its particularity, is always unique. Now, of course, the
French Revolution is no different in this from a fly falling to
the ground. Both are unique events, unlike any other. So what
distinguishes the French Revolution from a fly, from an itch
somebody has? It's unique, but it's *significantly* unique. Roy
Eckardt says the Holocaust is "uniquely unique," as you
probably have heard him say.

   HJC   In *Long Night's Journey into Day.*

   EF   Roy is getting more and more into wanting to be a
philosopher, but he hasn't spent his lifetime being a philosopher. He's spent his lifetime being a theologian. Of course,
theologians ought to have always known this. Though, of
course, they don't analyze it philosophically. When St. Augustine told the pagans of the dying and rising God, they said,
"We knew this all along. Gods are dying and rising all the
time." And he said, "No, Christ having risen, will die no
more." Now that's an event which is supposed to be
"uniquely unique," as Roy Eckardt would put it.

   I think the intention is good but not the formulation. It is
necessary to introduce the category of *significance*. If you are
a historian you have to distinguish between events that are
significant and events that are not. For example—referring to
a bad Jewish joke—a couple gets married, but it's been well-
known that they've had intercourse for a long time, and
people ask the question that a Jewish boy is supposed to ask
at the Seder, "How is this night different from every other
night?" However, assuming for the purpose of the argument
that there are still such things as marriage vows which are
taken seriously in a person's life, the wedding night is not
just unique, like scratching yourself on the back, but significantly unique. That is, as Roy Eckhardt would say, "uniquely
unique." But, as I would say, it's a *caesura* in your life. Suppos-
ing you believe, as I do, that marriage is a real commitment.
After the marriage vows are made, your life is different, her
life is different. To give another example, when our first child

was born, at least for me, my life changed, *everything* changed.

This is just by way of background, to establish what I mean by unique. And I think it is completely silly, when the Holocaust is being discussed, for people to throw in this red herring that every event is unique. This has vast philosophical implications. When I say, which I do, that no historian has succeeded and, I think, will ever succeed, in explaining the Holocaust adequately—this raises the whole problem of historical explanation as a philosophical problem. I've heard this many times: "You never explain a historical event completely"—except that in this case the most significant thing is the one which is hardest to explain. You've seen *Shoah* and you've read Hilberg—I think *Shoah* is an outstanding achievement, and Hilberg's, despite the reservation everybody has about what he says about the Jewish Councils, is an outstanding work. Now Hilberg had this to say: "I confine myself to the small questions for fear of giving too small an answer to the big question." Hilberg had once given a long seminar at the University of Toronto—two or three hours— about how they did it. He came over for coffee. And I said to him, "Raul, you've written more than anyone else about how they did it. Now you tell me the answer to the big question: Why did they do it?" And he heaved a big sigh and he said, "They did it because they wanted to do it." A tautology. I quoted this when I read a paper on the subject in the APA (American Philosophical Association). I expected great hostility, especially from the Jews. By arguing that the Holocaust is unique the Jews all are very defensive about the Holocaust—especially professors. But, to my surprise, it went over and one man got up and made a very good point. He said: "Hilberg shouldn't have said they *wanted* to do it, he should have said they *decided* to do it." Big difference. That was a big decision, indeed—and a unique one.

You flatten the Holocaust by making it a case of genocide. It does have things in common with others, but I think the most significant part about the Holocaust is what it doesn't have in common. Namely, that they made the decision that *not a single* Jew must stay alive. That wasn't done with the others. My point is not which is worse. I don't even raise that question. I just want to understand the Holocaust decision. And it means that I understand that you can't understand it. Why did they decide it? People have written a lot about historical explanation and philosophers. But no one has paid any attention to the Holocaust as a philosophical problem for historical explanation.

The English philosopher R.G. Collingwood, taking Caesar's crossing of the Rubicon as an example, tries to explain why Caesar did it. He asks what was in Caesar's mind. What reasons did he have? His reason was he had decided to take over Rome. And once a historian has given this reason, he has explained Caesar's action. Many people have raised objections to this because very few historical decisions are made by one individual. Many decisions are collective decisions. Many are things people stumble into. I think when the Germans sort of edged towards World War I, they had no idea what they let themselves in for. But in the Holocaust it is very clear that, at the Wannsee Conference or before, somebody *decided.* Every available Jew has to be murdered. Somebody decided it. Collingwood is dead now. If he were still alive I think he would say, "This is as good a case [as] I find in the history of decision-making." Somebody, or a group of people, making this decision. But in going to find the reason why they did it, he couldn't take it seriously, at face value. It's a rational decision for Caesar to try to take over the Roman Empire, but is it a rational decision for Hitler to decide that even if Germany goes down, every Jew has to be murdered? What kind of a decision is this? And if you consider Hitler's *Weltanschauung,* you have to ask: "Why should anybody have a crazy *Weltanschauung* such as this?" It doesn't make sense. I've tried to go through the historians. And when they say: "Well, the answer you have to give is Hitler really believed it," I can't take that at face value either.

I just had a long talk with Martin Gilbert, who is a great historian. And he confirmed my belief that Hitler was an actor. He showed historical evidence how, as an actor, he could fool people. I said to Gilbert, "You've got to write a book just about that." People would come to Hitler and he was such a consummate actor that he fooled people. He fooled McKenzie King, who came away from a meeting feeling that Hitler was a nice person. He certainly fooled Chamberlain. But the case I found unbelievable is that of a distinguished Jew from England who had a list of Jews who were in concentration camps and he was determined to confront Hitler with that list. And Hitler was well prepared for this. (He was always well prepared.) And he persuaded this man that he was the protector of the Jews and if it weren't for him, then things would be much worse for the Jews in Germany. So the man never pulled out his list. I said to Gilbert, "You've got to connect all those things." And the most shocking case was Lloyd George—nobody's fool. Lloyd George, I forget when it was, visited Hitler. And Hitler said to him, having done his research, "You've seen our Autobahn—I got the idea from you, from plans you had way back," and Lloyd George went away flattered. Now, a man who does that and who practices his speeches before the mirror and then gives them, acts sincerely. I'm not sure whether Hitler really believed what he practiced to the end of his days. I'm not sure. I mean, you get to such a situation—but if that's not a philosopher's problem, I really don't know what is. Because a philosopher wants to explain historical evidence, and here comes Hilberg, you know, very, very philosophically sound, and said, "I would give too small an answer." And Lanzmann did the same thing. Never once, in those hundred hours of interviews, did he ask any of the criminals interviewed, why did they do it? Because he would have gotten too small an answer. And you know, almost an amusing thing, the editor of *Midstream*—you probably know *Midstream* magazine.

HJC   Yes, Joel Carmichael.

EF   When I sent him an article on *Shoah*, he turned it down, partly because I did not criticize Lanzmann for never asking anyone why they did it. But then he published his own answer to the question—they were crazy! What kind of an explanation is this? That's much too small. If Hitler was

crazy, how come they let him run a whole country? Almost
conquer the world? Or were they all crazy? That doesn't
answer anything. So I think highly of Hilberg, who has spent
his whole life thinking about this and then says: "The big
question I will not try to answer." Carmichael gives much
too small an answer.

So this is for me a philosophical problem. You notice that
thus far I have not raised the Jewish issue at all. Now, if
somebody says, maybe there is a similar problem about Cambodia, I would reply that it is possible. I won't press the issue
of the Holocaust at this point. I do raise the problem. Can you
say about Cambodia, in reply to why they did it, [that] there is
a rational answer—á la Collingwood? Or can you say, in that
case, that the ideology explains it? The same thing with the
Gulag. I do understand similarities between that and the
Holocaust. I learned this from [Terence] Des Pres's beautiful
book about a horrible subject—the part about excremental
assault.

HJC   Yes, in *The Survivor.*

EF   Why did they perpetuate this excremental assault? I
think in order to make the facts fit the "theory." The theory
was that Jews are lice and dirty, so they had to make them
covered with excrement. Here I see a parallel to the Gulag.
Since their "theory" says that anybody in the worker's paradise who resists must be crazy, they had to treat them by
assault through psychiatry. And there may be similar paral-
lels with Cambodia. I am quite prepared to leave this open.

I do think, though, that it is entirely wrong to say: "Let's
forget about what's unique about the Holocaust. Let's forget
about the fact that they wanted to murder every single Jew.
Let's just deal with genocide-in-general." In that case, before
you know it, you compare the Holocaust to the fate of the
American Indians (which was quite different)! This has happened to me so many times.

When I gave this paper to the American Philosophical
Association, they publicized it and somebody accused me of
Jewish parochialism. He added that when they massacred
Indians these "good Christian murderers" said they had no

souls. This was important news to me, so I wrote back very, very softly. Still, I said that if I were not a Jew, I would have to say the same thing about the Holocaust. I maintained that there is still a difference. A fundamental difference, because you can understand why they wanted to get rid of Indians—they wanted to rob their land. But why did they want to get rid of Jews when this would involve digging their own grave—which it meant towards the end? Why the forced marches, for instance, towards the end of the war? It made no sense from their own point of view. Why didn't they just go off and leave those Jews to the Russians? Instead, the Nazis had to march with them and spend precious energy they needed for the defense—why this? These are the questions you have to ask and I think the other is just avoiding the problem. Now, with Cambodia: I read one thing about Cambodia which even the Nazis didn't think of, and I said that there is a problem for philosophy but I don't know enough about it. They apparently trained children to be sadistic toward their parents by making them torture animals first. I read this somewhere, and I said, well, the Nazis didn't think of that. That's a new one to me. But it still leaves the question whether the ideology, for the sake of which they did it, is intelligible. The Nazi ideology is not intelligible, and so on. I don't know whether Hitler believed it. Yet they did it to the bitter end.

Now, neo-Nazis say it never happened at all. The Communists say it did happen but to "victims of fascism," a propagandistic lie since only the Nazis had gas chambers and murder camps. Now this leftist escapism is taken further by Ernest Nolte with his "three faces of fascism." For him the Holocaust is a minor aspect of fascism—in general. But Italian fascism never planned murder camps for Jews or anyone else. (In fact, they protected Jews when the Nazis tried to abduct them.) And Nolte leaves Franco out? I guess Franco doesn't fit into his preconceptions. So I think the Holocaust is a problem for philosophy, when you add to this that it's not just for historical explanation but [for] what they did to human beings in Auschwitz. Both to the victims and to the

executioners. It threatens your whole accepted picture of
what man is. It's a large problem for philosophy.

HJC   Himmler recognized, didn't he, that there might be
some impact on the executioners?

EF   Oh, yes. And, of course, there was. It's an amazing
phenomenon that a fellow like Eichmann is a desk murderer
and then becomes an ordinary citizen. Never touches a fly
after that. So it's a new phenomenon for philosophy. Sometimes the murderers themselves didn't know why they did it.
There is this woman who interviewed Stangl.

HJC   Gita Serenyi.

EF   Yes. At one point she asked him, "Why did they do
it?" (She said "they" not "Why did you?" But if he wasn't
involved, who was?) And he said: "They wanted their
money." Now this is a completely absurd answer—they'd
already taken all their money. Here's the man who'd done it
and he doesn't know why he'd done it! Did he or Eichmann
never think about it? Hannah Arendt has an easy time saying
Eichmann is banal. Arendt was a philosopher, so I followed
her idea through in her writings—but she never followed it
through to its logical end herself, because to my knowledge
she never said Hitler was banal, never. So it comes to the old
thing, only Hitler runs everybody, and everybody else is banal. As for Hitler, he's crazy. So how come a crazy man
practically runs the world? We run around in circles.

Well, then Serenyi asked Stangl the next question—a very
good question—"If they were going to murder them anyway,
in the end, what was the point in all this infinite labor
involved in humiliating people and torturing them?" And he
said: "The purpose was to condition the murderers to do
what they did in the end. To brutalize them first." Serenyi
accepted that. But I think it's unacceptable. What is easier in
order to brutalize the murderer—just to order them to shove
people into the gas chambers and press a button, or to make
them, day in, day out, through ever more complicated forms
of torture, to the end of making them murder in the end
people they got to know? I think the second is much harder.

HJC   Well, some of the people authorized to torture and kill were not Nazis, were not even Germans. They were prisoners themselves.

EF Yes. So, you see, Stangl didn't understand what he himself was doing and, in this case, neither did Serenyi, despite the fact that she interviewed him day after day. And therefore the problem of what was really this, what I call, anti-world of the Nazi camp, is still a question for philosophers to consider. And the way I put it is this. My favorite philosopher is Hegel, except I think that if Hegel were alive today, his whole philosophy would have to be different. Hegel made a great joke—"Better bad weather than no weather at all." A wonderful joke. And a very profound one because bad weather means, still, a climate in which you can live. If there is no weather at all, then there is such a freezing cold that everybody dies. Hegel then went on from there and said: "Better a bad state than no state at all." Since he was not an anarchist but the opposite of an anarchist, even if you have bad laws, some sort of human life is possible even in a bad state. I think Hegel couldn't say this anymore today, because the murder camp was a state within a state. But it was geared not to life; it was geared to criminality and death. That institution, once having existed, is a horrible new blot on all future human history. For there is the danger that it serves as a precedent.

When I was in Berlin in 1985, the first time in forty-five years, I bought my first newspaper, and the front page story was as follows: A Jewish woman who's a survivor lives in Germany. One day she gets a parcel in the mail. She opens the parcel and it's ashes. She gets an anonymous phone call— "These are ashes from Auschwitz." The woman has a nervous collapse. She phones the police. They track down the fellow who did it. He is a young fellow she befriended, except one night he gets drunk and that's what he does. No wonder it made the front page. A new evil has been let loose in the world. You can't say it's over and done with. It's created a precedent. And this whole question of whether Auschwitz was a precedent for Cambodia, just as the Armenians were a precedent for Auschwitz, is a very deep question, not just for philosophers but also for historians to consider.

HJC Why is it, do you think, that so few philosophers are engaged in examining this problem?

EF There are several reasons. In fact, here I repeat myself from the paper I had in *The Journal of Philosophy* a couple of years ago. But I started out with this: first, philosophers always, almost, have a knee-jerk tendency to universalize— which is fair enough, in general. But they don't universalize about the French Revolution. Maybe some people would say, "Never mind the French Revolution. That's for historians. A philosopher should ask about revolutions in general." But at least a few examples of philosophers—to name just two, Hegel and Marx—thought the French Revolution was an epoch-making event and therefore unique and a precedent. (I don't think I can understand either Hegel or Marx without the view they take of the French Revolution as an epoch-making event. Of course, Marx thought it was only the first; a second one had to follow. But if they had believed that revolutions come and go and mankind always remains the same, both would have had different philosophies.)

Now, of course, one could go back to Aristotle, who says in "The Poetics" that history is less philosophical even than poetry. Because poetry is universal and describes something that could happen to everyone, whereas history is purely accidental and in the realm of contingency. So if you take the Aristotelian view, which of course has a long tradition, then the Holocaust merely illustrates man's inhumanity to man. (A nice platitude.) It's not that it isn't uniquely terrible, but what is unique about it is not a philosopher's business. But, especially now, very few philosophers take the Aristotelian view—feminist philosophy, black theology, and other phenomena bound up with history.

That is point number one. Point two also has a long philosophical tradition. This is that evil is unintelligible. This really goes back to Plato. And then, in Plotinus, [it] finds its greatest expression. I've always loved Plotinus; he may be

one of the greatest of ancient philosophers. And if you have
a concern with the Jewish and the Christian tradition, it is
no wonder to me that St. Augustine should have known
Plotinus. And the Jews had their Plato mediated through neo-
Platonism, which they loved because they too believed in one
God. But the way Plotinus reaches his view about evil (Plato
really before him), that evil is unintelligible, that to him is
the absence of the positive. In Plato, the idea of the good is
supreme, and what's evil? Evil is not a contrary reality but a
negation. Good is light and evil is darkness, and what is
darkness? Darkness is the absence of light. That's . . .

HJC   Evil is the absence of light.

EF   I think of one of my philosophical heroes in our time,
in fact a mentor, Leo Strauss. Leo Strauss influenced me very
deeply when I was a young student. Then, when I came to
North America and found the liberal rabbis were still living
with nineteenth-century optimism, I felt very much alone.
Then I developed a very close relationship with Strauss. Leo
Strauss was wonderful. He understood the horror of Nazism.
He had a choice of going either to Jewish thought or into
political philosophy. He became a very significant political
philosopher. Now he has got all sorts of posthumous influence and his conclusion—rightly or wrongly—was that
modern civilization went wrong from the very start. It went
wrong with the scientists trying to be morally neutral. He
went back to the Greeks, where moral neutrality did not
exist. To Plato, the world is unintelligible unless the idea of
the good is supreme. So, rightly or wrongly, this was Strauss'
position.

The reason why I bring up Strauss is that when he wrote
his memoir, he made one point on which I had to disagree
with him. He said, and I quote almost verbatim: "It is safer to
understand the low in terms of the high, than the high in
terms of the low. If you understand the high in terms of the
low, you will distort it. All nobility of character, you understand in terms of the 'id,' vanishes and you distort it." I agree
with that part of it. But what of the opposite? "If you look at
the low in terms of the high, it'll show itself in what it is."

That's going back to the Platonic view, in what he said about evil, perversion, distortion, following blind passion and all that. With that I disagree when it comes to the Holocaust. A philosopher has to look at it straight, even if it goes against his philosophical grain. The French Revolution is understood as epoch-inducing, as a part of the liberation of man. The Holocaust too is unique but starkly negative. No wonder philosophers find this hard to take. The Socratic answer is "evil is ignorance." That is not true about the Holocaust, for there were PhD's among the murderers. I suppose if you asked Strauss he would say: "Yes, but what kind of PhD's were those? They were not PhD's in the Platonic tradition." So it's an argument between us and I shall go on pondering it. But I do think it is necessary to look at evil in its own right, despite the fact that ultimately it's unintelligible. It's unintelligible theologically, too.

When I had my two-year scholarship for the book *To Mend the World*, I had to appear before a committee, a wonderful committee, and was asked, "Why are you doing this?" And I explained it and one of my colleagues, a philosopher, said: "Is this a new idea that evil is unintelligible?" I said: "It's as old as the beginning of the Bible. Why did Adam eat the apple? Because Eve tempted him. Why did Eve tempt him? Because the snake tempted her. But who tempted the snake?" So I think really, theologically, it is unintelligible, too. But you've got to confront it! Even if that means that ultimately your reason is shattered by it, and people like Theodor Adorno said the metaphysical capacity is shattered by the Holocaust—but then he didn't pursue it any further. That is the problem I have as a philosopher. And the same editor who persuaded me to write *What Is Judaism?* says: "Now you should write a book *What Is Philosophy?*" If I see him I'll tell him: "I hope you don't expect me to write an introduction to philosophy for the layman. I hope you mean that I should write about philosophy after the Holocaust has happened." I don't know whether I can do it, but before I make a commitment like that, I want to think it over. At least I want to know what he has in mind.

There is a third point I made in Washington, and I thought this would get the Jewish professors mad. Modern philosophy has an anti-Jewish bias. Especially when it's practiced by Jewish philosophers. They lean over backwards in not being "egocentric" by singling out the Jewish problem as though it deserved philosophical attention. So they won't talk about anti-Semitism but call it prejudice, or racism. But anti-Semitism and racism are not the same phenomenon. There is only one philosopher who wrote about anti-Semitism, *qua* philosopher, and that was Jean Paul Sartre. You don't get Jewish philosophers writing about anti-Semitism as such, because they don't want to be viewed as "parochial" about it. And modern philosophy has not been fair to the Jewish element and Jewish existence in modern civilization. So it is automatically assumed that if someone like me says that the Holocaust is "unique," that I'm guilty of Jewish parochialism.

At Pittsburgh Theological Seminary—it must have been in the late 60s, when it still wasn't known that I had become some terrible radical who takes the Holocaust seriously—I was still practicing old fashioned Jewish-Christian dialogue. And I was asked to give a speech on Revelation, and of course, it was well received and everything was very nice. But I was still reeling under the impact of the Six Day War. So I suggested: "How about getting together with the professors to talk about the Holocaust?" So we talked about it, and a professor got up and said, "Tell me, Rabbi" (whenever I am addressed like that I know something nasty is coming, because I haven't been a practicing rabbi in forty years), "do American Jews care about blacks at all?" So I said to him the standard thing: "None of us cares enough, but I think compared to Protestants and Catholics, American Jews have nothing to be ashamed of." Then when we walked out, one of his colleagues was full of rage but he didn't say it publicly. He said to me: "At least in America we have never wreaked a Holocaust on the blacks." Now, what I would tell any questioner today is this: "What makes you think they don't care? What except anti-Semitism can be responsible for this question? What makes you think I don't care about blacks?" But in nicer form, you still get this today. In fact, Franklin Littell told me only two days ago, one of the questions he gets all the time is, didn't he think that what the Israelis do to the Arabs is just the same thing that the Nazis did to the Jews. How can you compare the two? Of course all sorts of Jews will be apologetic. The first thing they do is they attack the invasion of Lebanon and have to outdo everybody else in doing this. So, the third element of philosophical neglect of the Holocaust is unconscious anti-Semitism and Jewish academic reluctance to be militant in fighting it.

HJC   Now, another subject you have written about is the relationship of the establishment of the State of Israel to the Holocaust. Some people see cause and effect, and you argue against that.

EF   Oh, yes. I should say just for the record, the second aspect, "In what respect is the Holocaust unique for Jews?" I didn't raise thus far in our discussion. That, of course, is really quite a separate question. And I didn't think it would be better to deal with the first question first, namely, "Is the Holocaust unique *per se*?" But whether it is unique for Jews raises all the religious and theological questions. I don't know whether you want to go into this now.

HJC   If you'd like, yes.

EF   The first question, the one already tackled, is, I think, in a way agonizing enough. I don't think the philosophers should ever sit in the Ivory Tower. They do have purely theoretical questions to answer. But there is a personally human aspect if you, as I do, arrive at the conclusion that, Socrates and Plato and Aristotle to the contrary notwithstanding, and Leo Strauss notwithstanding, there is no such thing as a permanent human nature, that man is a historical animal—I don't like the conclusion. It would be much better, much more comforting, to conclude that man has a permanent nature: that although a man can be perverted, man's nature cannot be destroyed—it's a permanent thing. Then, at least, you can conclude that after these horrors we can recapture the tradition of what is best in man. But if this is not the case, if the new horror is precedent—what happened once is a precedent for future things to come—then I think a philosopher cannot just stay in the academy but must also ask the question that moves Franklin Littell so much, and I'm sure moves you. What do we have to do after this has happened? It goes very, very deep, and people cast about for answers, and it's not so easy to come up with any. So the first question is painful enough. But still, compared to this, the Jewish question is much more agonizing. I had it asked yesterday, in fact, and got into an argument with a young boy, and my host said, "This guy's crazy." Well, I couldn't dismiss him as crazy. And that is, "What is a Jew who has a tradition of faith? What does he do after this has happened?" That is what concerned me all my life. In the first part of my career, I just pushed the Holocaust away. I wrote about evil in general, Nasizm in general, all of which was safe enough. But not until 1967 did I say anything about the Holocaust.

HJC   Because of the war?

EF   No, this actually was before the war. But this was just a coincidence. On Purim 1967, which coincided with Easter, I was invited to participate in a symposium with Elie Wiesel, and the subject was post-Holocaust Jewish values. I couldn't say "No" because my arm was twisted morally. One does have responsibilities. And I got sick. I had a typical case of psychological sickness. And the sickness vanished after the meeting was over. Because, how can you have those two things together—a perpetuation, in fact a rejuvenation, of the Jewish faith and a confrontation of the Holocaust? That is what has really been my lifelong agony. You can't play down the Holocaust in order to rescue the Jewish faith. First, it's untrue, and second it is an insult to the victims. On the other hand, if a Jew confronts the Holocaust and ends up in despair, he hands Hitler a posthumous victory. That was a concern in 1967 and has been my central concern ever since—my most basic concern as a Jewish religious thinker.

In 1967 I stated the problem, but maybe I shouldn't say I came up with a solution. Still, I said the only thing that ever became famous—a 614th commandment, that Jews are forbidden to give Hitler posthumous victories. Yet, the way this has been distorted, and even ridiculed by some just shows how little they want to face the problem. But I stated very precisely, in print, several times, what my problem was. And why I thought the 614th commandment was necessary. It was not enough to resort to the old imagery of evil—Amalek, Pharoah, and Haman—for a qualitatively new evil had been loosed on the religious world of Judaism. And this is perhaps the most agonized sentence I ever wrote: "Sometimes in the nineteenth century, European Jews brought a child sacrifice by the mere minimum commitment to the Jewish faith, the bringing up of Jewish children. But, unlike Abraham, they didn't know what they were doing, and there was no re-prieve." I am driven more and more to the conclusion that what the Nazis were trying to do was not only kill the Jewish people but kill the faith of the survivors as well, ever after. The dilemma arising from this attempt I had stated very clearly, and I restated it when the *Religious Studies Review* asked me to summarize my work. [See July, 1987 issue. See also the preface to the second edition of *To Mend the World* (1989).] Never before was a Jew in a situation where the possibility existed that the distant offspring of him might be killed for no other reason than *his* decision, right now, to bring up Jewish children. It is morally impossible [for him] to be implicated in murder, or the very possibility of murder. Therefore, if, nevertheless, I have Jewish children, I am impli-cated in the possibility of murder. But if I cannot do that and therefore I will have no Jewish children, I do my share not only in making an end to the Jewish people but also the Jewish faith. So therefore, collectively speaking, the Jew after Hitler is either a potential murderer or a potential suicide. And it is in response to *that* dilemma that I said, "We are forbidden to grant Hitler posthumous victories."

Now, the "learned" theologians who attacked me never seem to have read this statement, because they proceeded as though posthumous victories for Hitler were impossible. For instance, Michael Wyshcogrod is a very intelligent philoso-pher but he only shows that [a] man can be that and still talk like a fool. In a New York symposium, Elie Wiesel participated, as did Yitz Greenberg and Wyshcogrod, and I. Later Wyshcogrod published his remarks and later still Gene Borowitz, another intelligent thinker, supported him. Wyshcogrod wrote: "If some mad dictator wanted to kill all stamp collectors, you would, of course, have to stop him. But this wouldn't mean that we had to become stamp collectors." So when I answered, I said: "This reminds me of what a professor of mine used to say, 'When you go to Harvard, they don't cure you of your stupidity, they make a system out of it.'" I told him: "You overlooked a small point. There hasn't been a two-thousand-year history of mad dictators trying to kill stamp collectors." So it shows how a man can be intelligent and yet be foolish. Because not only was my problem that there could be posthumous victories of Hitler, which are there anyway, all the while—the Neo-Nazis, the Arab states, encouraged by Hitler's success, trying to destroy Israel, etc. The way I have stated the dilemma between implications in collective Jewish murder and collective Jewish suicide, Hitler's posthumous victory seemed not only possible but inevitable. And I said simply: "No this is not allowed. Even if we don't know yet how to avoid it, it is not allowed." And everything else really came later.

And when I then asked *what constitutes* giving Hitler a posthumous victory? I made four judgments. That was also ignored. (Later on, some ultra-leftists said: "Israel's giving Hitler a posthumous victory by oppressing Palestinians." And some ultra-rightists said: "Israel is giving a posthumous victory to Hitler by *not* oppressing Palestinians"—Meir Kahane, for example.) But what I said has been invoked by all sorts of people, without confronting the dilemma from which it arises, with which I started in the first place. Judgments are necessary to apply the 614th commandment. In 1967 I made judgments, but since 1967 I have become more cautious. I said then four things. We mustn't forget the victims. We must survive. We must not despair of mankind, which is the ethical element. Finally, four, we mustn't despair of God. Now I've become much more hesitant since, for instance, Richard Rubinstein, whom I'm sure you know . . .

HJC Yes, and I know you criticized his work here in this book.

EF Yes, and Rubinstein was shot at by many people saying: "You are giving Hitler a posthumous victory." And I met him a number of times, and I disagree with him. But I think to shoot that command at him is unfair. What am I going to say to a man who despairs after this? Am I really going to say: "You give Hitler a posthumous victory"? You get into great difficulties when you descend from the general to the particular. And in this, I think, I am in good company. When Kant formulated his categorical imperative ("act as though you could universalize the maxim") that was fine. I have no quarrel with that. But when it comes to specifying, Kant himself got into trouble. He wrote a silly essay. No less a philosopher than *Kant wrote a silly essay.* Over the presumable right to lie. The general principle is: if everybody habitually lied, nobody would ever be believed. Therefore your purpose in lying is to be believed. You have no right to lie. Fine as far as that goes. But now you ask: "Are there ever any circumstances where you have not only the right to lie, but maybe even the duty to lie?" And Kant was silly when he said, "No." He spoke against his own better judgment. Because, obviously—and I always used to tell my students—if somebody is running, and the guy comes after him with a knife, and he asks me "Where did he go?" I have *a duty* to lie to him. But Kant was afraid: what if everybody said that? So he wrote a silly essay. I've heard so many times, what if everybody said his own "Holocaust" is unique? That is a false question. The right question is, what if everybody *in the same circumstances* said this of *his* "Holocaust"? This means, of course, that you have to make a judgment, and judgments are fallible. (Also, you have to know the facts.)

Now, Sartre had moved from the eighteenth to the twentieth century. He wrote some good stories. This is a symbolic story, but it could really have happened. Some resistance fighters are caught by the Nazis. They are threatened with torture unless they tell where their friends are hidden. So they think: "We'll tell them the wrong place, and by the time

they come back we'll have committed suicide, because we
can't stand the torture, we would give them away." Except
the absurdity that their friends had moved from their hiding
place to the very "wrong" place they had given to the Nazis
and get caught. This is the kind of story which Kant would
never have taught of in his nicer times. You have to make a
judgment sometimes in an absurd world. Which is why you
cannot be absolutely sure of making the right judgment.

I think it was Daniel Silver, in an article in *Judaism* a while
back, who wrote that the 614th commandment is valid, but
that it is empty of content until you make a judgment. Quite
true, but what he did not know or remember is that back in
1967 I myself made my judgments. Since then, as I say, I have
become much more cautious. I then said that a Jew mustn't
despair of the world, and a former student of mine took this
to mean that a Jew must care about everyone's problems
except his own. That's a distortion, and sooner or later it
leads to the lie that Israel is losing her soul. Maybe the
worriers about Israel's soul might worry a bit about Israel's
body, especially if they are located at Berkeley or some similar place! These are difficult times to live with in Israel. I
think anyone who makes a judgment and says, "I'm the only
one who's right because I speak with direct authority from
heaven," I think he's bound to be wrong. On a matter like this
a man like Reinhold Niebuhr has been a teacher of us all. You
remember him attacking Christian pacifism. He says that
there is a time to be a pacifist and a time to not be a pacifist.
To be a pacifist vis-à-vis Hitler was morally wrong. Equally
wrong is a Christianity that teaches—to be sarcastic for a
moment—that Jews should turn the other cheek, when Jews
are at bay in Jerusalem [and] while they [Christians] dwell
safely in Babylon.

HJC I want to ask about the relationship that you've
written about between the Holocaust and the establishment
of the state of Israel. You say that there's not a cause and
effect relationship there.

EF No, I think the cause and effect relationship leads to
absurd and ultimately horrifying consequences. I've written

about this a little in *What Is Judaism* (1987). Suppose we start
out with this: Herzl attended the Dreyfus trial in Paris. (The
history is a bit more complicated than we generally assume,
but I'm not a historian. The fact seems that Herzl was already
a bit of a Zionist before the Dreyfus trial!) But the common
story is: he was an assimilated Jewish journalist until he got
to the Dreyfus trial, and the explosion of anti-Semitism and
the judicial murder converted him to Zionism. Is there a
simple cause and effect relationship there? In *What Is Judaism?* I proceed as follows. Presumably there were other Jewish journalists in Paris. It didn't have the same effect on *them*!
Some may have said, leaning over backwards, "I'm supposed
to report the trial and ignore the anti-Semitism." Another
Jewish assimilationist journalist, this one really chicken-
hearted, may actually have thought: "Who knows—maybe
Dreyfus is guilty! How do I know?" And some others, more
chicken-hearted still, may have felt that it was Dreyfus' own
fault. Why did he push himself in the anti-Semitic French
officer corps? He should have had the decency to convert to
Christianity first! Now on Herzl, this wasn't the effect.
Therefore, we cannot speak of cause and effect at all. We *can*
speak of challenge and response. "Response" means you *do*
something about the challenge, you *react* to it, you are a free
agent. If you go the "cause-effect" way, to "effect" of the
cause "Holocaust," then you end up with the obscenity and
the lie that the grandfather of the state of Israel was not Herzl
but Hitler. And this seems to be implied in what's-his-name's
novel. Why can't I remember his name? *The Portage [To San
Cristobal of A.H.]*.

    HJC   George Steiner.

    EF   Steiner, yes. I met Steiner on several occasions. He's
an extraordinary brilliant man, but not without great perver-
sity. He once asked us, my wife and me, "How many passports have you got?" I said, "What do you mean? Just one
passport!" He said, "You're a fool. A Jew, after what happened, should have four passports." Now we have got two
passports—one Israeli, the other Canadian. But we shall seek
no others. Last time Steiner was in Israel—he likes to bait

people and so tried to show that Diaspora Jewish existence is superior to Israeli. Why? Well, in the Diaspora there are so many great Jewish chess players. Where are the chess players in Israel? Jews used to be such great journalists—now Israeli journalism is mediocre. And finally—his climactic point— how many Nobel Prizes have the Technion professors won? Touché, you know. I wasn't at the meeting. If I had been there, I would have known what to reply. Not that I want to denigrate the Nobel Prize winners, but after we had a time in which even Nobel Prize winners, if they were Jews, were murdered, something had to be changed by Jews themselves, and it was the Israelis and not the Nobel Prize winners who did it. There is some sickness about Steiner. He reacts to the Holocaust by wanting to have four passports. That means he understands well enough what happened, and I suppose if he'd had four passports when he was in Germany—he was a child then—he would have got into one country or another. Is *that* the kind of change that suffices?

There is a certain sickness about Steiner's novel also—I couldn't stand finishing it. But the last word is given to Hitler, and he says that if it weren't for me you Jews wouldn't have your state. However, Steiner and PLO propagandists notwithstanding, the grandfather of the State of Israel was not Hitler. All the people who say this nicely ignore the fact that if Hitler hadn't been there, we wouldn't have a Jewish population problem in Israel—there would be six million more Jews who could have been potential immigrants. Not to mention all sorts of other things that would have been different—and better.

I try to picture myself as a survivor in a D.P. camp, and the natural thing to do is to wait until somebody will take me. Preferably, some nice country where I can forget. And most people did this. But then there were some who said, "After this, that's not enough," and they broke through the legal niceties of the postwar world and, through "illegal" ways, made their way to Palestine. (Yehuda Bauer wrote a book about it.) Now, when you look at these D.P.s, would you call them an "effect"? The effect would have been to be so totally demoralized as to be driven to suicide. But for these D.P.s to take this, of all times, to say: "Now we start a new page in Jewish history and it is on account of what has happened"— that is *not* an "effect." That is a *response* to a challenge—the greatest response to the greatest challenge the Jewish people has had in recent centuries.

This is on the human level. Now let me say a word about the religious level. When they decided to establish a state, how could Jews ever hope hope to succeed against such odds that they could do it on their own? So, therefore, in my own mind, I say of secularist Israelites that they behave as though they believed in God. On the other hand, the religious, (the ones that count to me are not those ultra-orthodox, but the ones who are prepared to serve in the army when throughout the Diaspora a Jew was supposed not to do this sort of thing and trust in God) they act as though you couldn't count on God—and, after the Holocaust, you can't. So I find that what ought to unite them is much stronger than what so often separates them. If I tell Yehuda Bauer, who doesn't believe in God, that he behaves as though he did, he doesn't object and sometimes we call him, jocularly, "Rabbi Bauer."

HJC I didn't know that. I'll have to call him that the next time I see him.

EF My wife particularly enjoys this. The first time we came to his kibbutz, we liked everything about it and I told him there was only one thing I missed, a synagogue. And at that time he did not give the characteristic Marxist answer but said: "If the rabbinate were not behaving as it did maybe there might be one"—or words to that effect. And then he showed me the material they use on Passover, and I found it a bit amusing because it's very difficult to have scriptural verses and leave God out.

The first time we came to Israel it was because we had been invited by Levi Eshkol. That was Elie Wiesel's doing, incidentally. Elie said: "They always invite politicians and money-givers and never thinkers. I'll do something about it." And he did. We arrived and within half an hour we got into a theological argument. They had a taxi there for us and the taxi driver's name was Elijah. And within a few minutes, he said, "I know you talk about miracles. But we don't believe in miracles." I replied in my broken Hebrew, "There are no miracles without human action." He said, "That I can accept." So at the first moment, we had this encounter. I think that ought to be the basic Israeli reality, and at high points and low points it is.

HJC Well, I wonder if something you've written about this may be the bridge. Not the secularism of the Jews, not the religiousness of the Jews, but the mystical, if you will, madness of the Jews in the face of history—particularly recent history—to continue to be a Jew is mad in the healthy sense.

EF The greatest thing I'm now wrestling with is for a book I'm writing to be called *The Jew of Today and the Jewish Bible*. I gave some lectures on this at Manchester University. Buber wrote an essay in 1926 called "The Man of Today and the Jewish Bible," and mine is deliberately an allusion to Buber: if he wrote it today, he could no longer use this title. Who was his "man" of today? He was a Central European intellectual, whether Jewish or Christian. Now he is no longer the center of the universe, and even if he were, a Jew is not merely a subspecies of him because he's been singled out by the Holocaust and then he singled himself out by founding a Jewish state. How does he read the Jewish Bible in this new situation? One chapter focuses entirely on a single passage which is on the wall of the house of the president of Israel in Jerusalem, and it's from Ezekiel, and says to the effect that God will gather the dispersed and bring them back to the land. In my book I don't ask what this passage means messianically. I don't ask what it means in the mind of Ezekiel, or in the mind of Christians. All I want to know is what it means as inscribed on that wall. In other words, how it applies to the State of Israel.

In the preceding chapter I am forced to the conclusion [that] if salvation came again to the Jewish people in our time, it came too late. This forced me to the admission that a salvation that came too late once could come too late again. Therefore, I cannot give messianic significance to the State of Israel. Precariousness is a built-in feature. And then I turn to the death and resurrection symbolism, also in Ezekiel, and have to admit that the Holocaust smashed the symbolism. The only thing that has been resurrected then is hope. And then I came—this is quite amazing to me—to what should have been an evident discovery. The *Hatikva* uses the words from Ezekiel, with the dead bones saying "our hope is lost"— and our hope is *not* "lost." And what I say is that when Naftali Imber wrote those words in the nineteenth century, he could have had no idea what they would mean one day. And, what's more, we still don't know what they mean because events have not sunk in even yet. This is my most recent way of coping with what has happened and is happening. On the one hand hope has been resurrected, but on the other, it is flawed. What justifies hope in this world? We talked about this before. Have you got much hope for the world? And yet, by virtue of this same "madness" or whatever you call it, Jews are not only committed to hope but also the witnesses of it to the world. There can't be today any hope that is just passive and not joined up with action, either for the Jews or [for] the world, to which they are witnesses.

HJC Without seeming too simplistic, can I understand one sign of your hope being your decision to live in Israel?

EF Yes. And, you know, it's a mixture of hope and action. Finally I'm writing down my memoirs. At least I'm thinking of writing them. And the one part I have almost finished is "At Home in Toronto," but that really ended in '67. And the next part of living in Canada I call "Between Toronto and Jerusalem," because when the Six Day War showed that the world hasn't really changed and [that] the Christians once again were silent and a Holocaust might happen again, this time in Israel, from that moment on, we really wondered whether it wasn't our duty to be where the central action is. Because I'm convinced, unfortunately, that if, God forbid, the state of Israel were to go down, that would be the end of

Jewish history after four thousand years. As for the Jewish faith, all the questions people raise are really minor compared to that. I am still more at home in Toronto than in Jerusalem but have just explained why, in this historic moment, Jerusalem is where I feel I ought to be.

ELIE WIESEL

Elie Wiesel was awarded the Nobel Peace Prize in 1986 and has been nominated for the Nobel Prize in Literature several times. As artist and activist, writer and peacemaker, he was recognized for his works on behalf of Jewish Holocaust survivors, Cambodians, victims of apartheid, Central American refugees, persecuted Baha'is in Iran, the starving in Ethiopia, and the Miskito Indians in Honduras.

Born in Romania, Elie Wiesel endured Auschwitz and Buchenwald as a teenager. After the war, he settled first in France, then worked as a United Nations correspondent for an Israeli newspaper, and finally settled in the United States. His published works number over thirty books, including perhaps the best known memoir of the Holocaust, *Night* (1958). Among his novels are *Dawn* (1960), *The Accident* (1961), and *The Fifth Son* (1985). His nonfiction volumes include *The Jews of Silence* (1966), *Souls on Fire* (1972), *Five Biblical Portraits* (1981), and *Sages and Dreamers* (1991). He has also written dramas and cantatas. Included among his many awards are one hundred eighteen honorary degrees from colleges and universities in the United States, Israel, France, and Finland. He also received the Congressional Gold Medal of Achievement, the Humanitarian Award for the International League of Human Rights, the International

Brotherhood Award of the Congress of Racial Equality, and numerous other honors. He lives in New York and is professor of religious studies and of philosophy at Boston University.

HJC What impact do you think the Holocaust has had on the world?

EW It has had a tremendous impact, even more than we know and less than we expected. Today it serves as a point of reference, as a vantage point. It has become the epitome of evil, of cruelty. Whenever people want to say something about the impossibility of terrible things that *are* possible, they mention the Holocaust. On the other hand, I had anticipated an existential change, a total mutation. I thought that, somehow, after the event, the human condition would be different to a degree that we would all paradoxically benefit from its lessons. Still, the impact is great and it may even become greater in the future, after a few generations. It's like a time bomb; it takes time for the bomb to explode. It *will* explode in the consciousness of people. But my real fear is the trivialization of the experience. I am not afraid any more that it will be forgotten. I think many of us (including you and me) have done—not enough but we have tried to make sure that the story will not be forgotten. We have worked for memory. We have worked for the remembrance of things past and lives lost. Now I am afraid of trivialization. To trivialize the memory would be as tragic as the forgetting itself. You know, "kitsch" frightens me. It isn't new—we have spoken about it often, you and I, for so many years. The films, the television programs, the books, even certain meetings—all of a sudden everybody has something to say, and everybody says it with certainty, and everybody *knows* everything. Think of the generalizations, the theories, the systems that have come up! I believe that to remember is a sacred mission and, therefore, one must be worthy of the mission; one must be equipped and be ready for it. Not anyone—and not everyone—has the right to declare, to say, "I became a Holocaust scholar," or "Holocaust historian," or "Holocaust writer." It's not given to everyone. You must be worthy of it. Unfortunately, these days, because the subject is so popular, all kinds of people have entered the field and they desecrate the Temple.

HJC What a risk that is. It is like becoming a minister by ordaining yourself. It has to be done but it takes a lot of humility and good judgment.

EW Exactly. That's the first word that comes to mind: "humility." It takes humility to become aware of what happened and to become involved with what happened. I don't feel the humility in those persons. People today speak about it with such arrogance—the arrogance of false knowledge—that I wonder whether it would not have been better *not* to have so many people involved in so many plans, so many programs, so many projects, so many buildings.

HJC What would you like government to do?

EW First of all, to make a greater effort in the field of education. It is clear that contemporary history must become part of the curriculum. But in order for the subject to be properly taught to high school students you need good teachers. Therefore, special programs must be developed and prepared and financed for special teachers. If not, the effort would be counterproductive. If a teacher is boring in other subjects, and will also teach this subject boringly, then why teach? I would also like the government to observe once a year a remembrance day. I obtained this from President Carter. What makes me feel a little rewarded for my experience in Washington is the annual Day of Remembrance, which has now become a tradition—not only in Washington but in many state capitols, in city halls. Every community should know that once a year the victims of the Holocaust must be remembered.

HJC What can individuals do?

EW First of all, learn, read, absorb, and start again. Also, since individuals means husbands, wives, parents, they should think about the children—how to deal with the subject in front of their children. It is clear that not every hour is the right hour for the child to learn about it. So the parents should be aware, careful, but committed. They must know that the Holocaust can, and will, sensitize their children. In learning of past tragedies, they would grow to be sensitive, not only to the horror and the sparks of light that characterized that event, but also to the morality or immorality of our own life. Because of what they would learn about Treblinka, they should be more generous to those who need their generosity. Because they learn of the hunger that the victims were subjected to, they should feed the hungry. Because they would learn of the sick who were sentenced to death, because they were sick in all kinds of death camps, they should feel more compassion toward the sick in our own hospitals. Because they read about the uprooted communities in Eastern and Western Europe, they should feel more empathy with the homeless. So the subject has direct applications as well as immediate implications.

HJC   It would seem to be easier to make the applications where the tragedy occurred. And yet we have Romania, and Poland, and Hungary, and the Soviet Union now, where anti-Semitism is on the increase.

EW   That is truly one of the great disappointments. I know rationally that I am wrong. Already in 1945 there was anti-Semitism in Eastern Europe. The pogrom in Kielce was not the only one. There were others too, in Poland. They were of lesser dimensions, that is why they didn't make the newspaper. Antek Zuckerman, I think, wrote about them in his posthumous memoirs. There were many violent incidents in Hungary and Romania—when the Jews came back, they were met with hatred by those who had occupied the Jewish dwellings. They didn't want to let the surviving Jews back into their homes. In Russia we know what happened. The anti-Semitism was there and is still there. Even in Western Europe—why is it on the rise? Anti-Semitism is a kind of disease that accompanied our people, the Jewish people, for centuries and centuries. How to eradicate it? We should be able to undertake a huge operation to unmask the ugliness of anti-Semitism and then to disarm it. Then, hopefully, to uproot it.

HJC   Many writers who survived and wrote about the

Holocaust have committed suicide: Celan, Borowski, Levi, Amery, most recently Kosinski, and others. What does this mean? Have they seen something we don't see?

EW I think they saw the impotence of language. We've talked about it, we know it exists. The limits of language. Only writers realize that. Writers live because they write. Holocaust writers realize that their writing is not what they want it to be. Their disappointment is profound, metaphysical. It's not simply because they were in a bad mood or depressed. It's not something that the psychiatrist can cure, or that psychoanalysis can dissipate. It is a more profound malaise. It has divine implications. Where language fails, what can be its substitute? Usually it is action—activity, politics, violence, revolution. But, when the writers are not revolutionaries, and they don't believe in violence, what other outlet is there for them—except the ultimate violence, which is death?

HJC What is God doing?

EW I hope that he is not laughing. That has been my anguished obsession since my adolescence. Andre Neyer phrased the old question better than we did when he said: "What if all this is a question that God is asking of us?" God is entitled to that. "What are you doing with my creation? What are you doing with the world? What are you doing with yourself?" That doesn't dispense Him, that doesn't absolve Him from his responsibility. I believe God *is* responsible if God wants me to be responsible. Just as God is responsible for me, I may be responsible for Him. There again we reach the common ground, which is responsibility. Where does mine begin? Where does His end? Or is it the same responsibility? In other words, the question remains a question: What is God doing? I don't know. What does He want? What does He want to prevent, to obtain, to change? Why all that? If I knew, maybe I would stop writing—I don't know.

HJC An age-old question revolves around the apparent opposition of contemplation versus action. I am not sure that they are exclusive. But with meditation, prayer, there has to be some value in that.

EW   There is a value, but contemplation in the ancient mode was a mediation of oneself, implying, of course, God's presence. But it began and ended with oneself. That's why the monks entered the caves, and that's why prophets may have gone to the desert, and the ascetic dreamers were dreaming about their own salvation. I believe in contemplation/meditation only if it is a split contemplation. The self contemplating on the self. If I ask myself questions involving myself it is valid only if all of these interrogations involve an other self: if I do it *for* someone else. If I do it for myself, I'm sure it will end up in a precipice. But if I go on with contemplative endeavors, thinking that's what's happening to me may be of assistance to another, then the contemplation itself may have a deeper meaning.

ABOUT THE
INTERVIEWER

Harry James Cargas, professor of literature and language at Webster University in St. Louis, has among his twenty-five books: *Death and Hope* (1970), *Encountering Myself* (1977), *When God and Man Failed* (1981), *The Holocaust: An Annotated Bibliography* (1985), *Reflections of a Post-Auschwitz Christian* (1989), *Shadows of Auschwitz: A Christian Response to the Holocaust* (1990), and *Conversations with Elie Wiesel* (1992).

He has served as vice-president of the Annual Scholars' Conference on the Church Struggle and the Holocaust; on the Board of Directors of the Catholic Institute for Holocaust Studies; on the International Advisory Council for the Foundation to Sustain Christian Rescuers; on the Executive Council for the International Philosophers for the Prevention of Nuclear Omnicide; and on the Advisory Board of the Institute for Ultimate Reality and Meaning. He is the only Roman Catholic ever appointed to the International Advisory Committee of Yad Vashem in Jerusalem.

Cargas received the Tree of Life Award of the Jewish National fund (5,000 trees planted near Jerusalem in what is named the Harry James Cargas Parkland), the Eternal Flame

Award of the Anne Frank Institute, and the Human Rights
Award of the United Nations Association. He has lectured in
Berlin, Paris, Toronto, Rome, London, Vienna, Dublin, and
throughout the United States. He hosted a television program for the Central Education Network for several years and
has had a radio commentary program in St. Louis for over
eighteen years. Most recently he was appointed to the advisory board of the Romani-Jewish Alliance.